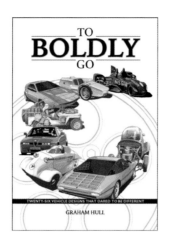

TO
BOLDLY
GO

TWENTY-SIX VEHICLE DESIGNS THAT DARED TO BE DIFFERENT

GRAHAM HULL

www.veloce.co.uk

First published in March 2017 by Veloce Publishing Limited, Veloce House, Parkway Farm Business Park, Middle Farm Way, Poundbury, Dorchester DT1 3AR, England.
Fax 01305 250479 / e-mail info@veloce.co.uk / web www.veloce.co.uk or www.velocebooks.com.
ISBN: 978-1-78711-002-1; UPC: 636847010027.

TO
BOLDLY
GO

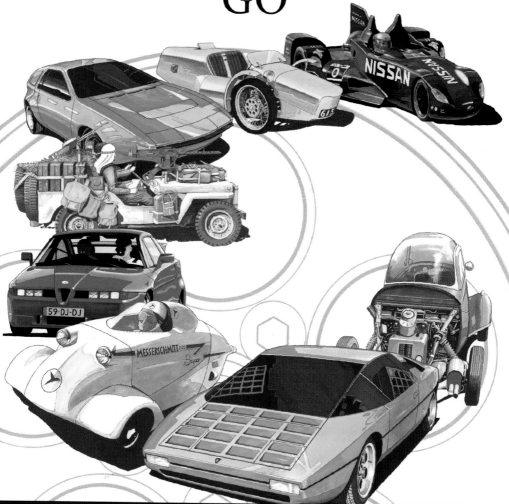

TWENTY-SIX VEHICLE DESIGNS THAT DARED TO BE DIFFERENT

GRAHAM HULL

VELOCE PUBLISHING
THE PUBLISHER OF FINE AUTOMOTIVE BOOKS

CONTENTS

PREFACE & INTRODUCTION

Dedicated to enthusiasts

Logic will get you from A to B.
Imagination will take you everywhere.

Albert Einstein

PREFACE

As well as the diversity and span of the vehicles studied in this book, the decision to include artwork, rather than photographs, is the result of no little thought. Taking the time to execute drawings or renderings, if nothing else, reflects on a level of enthusiasm for the subjects. Some knowledgeable devotees may recognise a particular number plate or vehicle, but hopefully any liberties taken can be covered by artistic licence. The Messerschmitt Tg500 engine, for instance, is based on the vehicle I owned that never had the 'rare-as-hens'-teeth' four-pipe exhaust system shown. After finishing the rendering, someone sent me a photo showing the complete system, which incorporated expansion cones going into the silencers, and these of course had to be added. A couple of vehicle colours have been changed for effect, but the images are true to period.

All of the renderings, for better or worse, are mine, except for three significant ones from personal heroes. The cutaway Bond Bug is by Lawrence Watts, whose family kindly gave permission for his typically superb illustration to appear. In the Tg500 Chapter are two drawings that Ian Kennedy did for me. Ian is unsurpassed as an illustrator/artist, whether in black and white or colour, contributing to the *Eagle* comic, Commando Comics, *Air Ace*, War Picture Library, and many more. The whole field of illustration is a genre of enthusiasm in its own right.

Enthusiasm is a constant backdrop to the 26 vehicles featured, the majority having one or more dedicated or associated clubs, and the remainder followed with great interest, as evidenced by internet traffic. All of these interested parties hold a wealth of information, which have contributed one way or another to the chapters. I would particularly thank the Panhard et Levassor Club GB and the Messerschmitt Owners' club, also my ex Rolls-Royce and Bentley colleague Martin Bourne, who checked things through and suggested that the 1950s were not totally grey.

INTRODUCTION

All design is a compromise, a balance of often contradictory requirements. For a product to be commercially successful it has to appeal to the greatest number of potential customers; therefore designers aim for the centre of the market opportunity. With motor cars this often leads to the 'all cars look the same' jibe, which, although not really true, is understandable, as all vehicles in a given class are trying to do the same job. 'Design by committee' is another accusation, but again it's inevitable that, in large organisations with huge responsibilities, the various disciplines unite to agree on the way forward. Conversely, radical or 'blue sky' designs are invariably the result of one person, or small group of enthusiasts, pursuing their ideal. Such projects are often labelled 'left of field,' 'off the wall,' 'skunk works,' 'marching to the beat of their own drum,' and so on.

Design, especially of vehicles, gets very interesting when dealing with the niches of extreme luxury, speed, or economy: all areas in which to look for innovation. Some endeavours, by definition, will not guarantee success, commercial or otherwise, but tend to be memorable in their own way.

Designers have their favourite cars – many appearing regularly in compilations of the most beautiful or important cars ever. Most would agree with the choices; however, over the years, another group of vehicles may appeal in a sometimes quirkier, though nevertheless fascinating, way. Some of them are beautiful; some not, but all are conceived and built with a purpose and commitment not always apparent in mass-produced vehicles. Some were produced in respectable numbers; others as one-offs never intended for the showroom, but all achieved their aim with a dash of flair and charisma. The motoring world would be a poorer place without them.

Qualification for inclusion

The designs chosen may, at first glance, appear a somewhat random, even eccentric, collection, and are all, I confess, from my personal scrapbook, but hopefully the images and descriptions will intrigue and fascinate, as they have this fan.

As with music, time has to pass before one can assess and catalogue designs that have survived the passage of time and remain potent. There are three from the 1930s; the majority are from the 1950s through to the 1970s; one is from the late 1980s, and one is from 2013. Recent developments are, of course, important and interesting, but road and racing machines basically came of age during the middle years of the period covered. Wealth and leisure time increased, and with it the love of personal expression, transport and motorsport. The fact that vehicles are improving year-on-year does nothing to detract from the originality and spirit of the vehicles featured here from across the decades. Several of the examples are included because they inspired individuals in significant number to use or modify them in a way not originally intended. Various designs were recognised as having potential that their manufacturers completely missed: Sir Alec Issigonis' Mini being the classic example, possessing a performance potential that the younger motoring public immediately responded to. The British Motor Corporation, making an economy car for families, was bemused by this unforeseen phenomenon. The Mini's profound mechanical legacy is at least equalled by 'added value' customising by owners, that became mainstream fare. This element shouldn't be overlooked by sociologists – it sounds pompous, but it's true.

One second-guesses what might appeal to others, but every example here will have its followers. Many designs have pretty much gone underground, occasionally appearing at auction, but usually passing from one devotee to another – effectively off the market and beyond rational estimate of their financial value. All the production cars included have owners' clubs, whose members have had to come to terms with the elevated prices of vehicles and spares, that, in some cases, were once almost given away.

The various vehicles featured should be given the reflection their creators deserve: they were all trailblazers in their way. Ultimately, we are talking about pure enthusiasm, one of our most underrated and precious attributes, a kind of benign attraction towards an inanimate object that projects a certain appeal – at least give the Bond Minicar a hearing! True enthusiasm attracts none of the seven deadly sins, except perhaps pride (okay, maybe envy, too), because devotees are just as enthused by others' achievements as their own. Enthusiasm, at its best, is one of the rare states of human experience that is largely selfless. The designs shown are the result of a passion for joint endeavour, such as concept cars, solutions to a niche market, and individual quests for fulfilment, like modified production cars, or radical racing cars. The individuals involved are never happier than when sharing and comparing notes with the like-minded, witnessed by countless gatherings of enthusiasts and their vehicles: hopefully the following pages reflect that.

A designer's viewpoint

When I was being trained as an industrial designer, a tutor explained that most people appreciate music without being able to play a note; likewise most people appreciate design with little understanding of the design process. Design has to meet several criteria: can it be made, does it do its job, is it affordable, and does it look good? The answer to this last question, of course, runs from 'okay' to 'wanting to lick it' – according to Steve Jobs of Apple Computers.

The creations of musicians and designers are often judged on face value, but some degree of knowledge of a product's engineering rationale always adds to one's appreciation. This is especially true of the vehicles contained in this book.

Of the 26 examples in this collection, all of them, to a greater or lesser degree, balance appearance with practicality. The balance percentage swings greatly between, say, the Willys Jeep and the British Leyland Zanda exercise, but both follow rules that any designer will recognise. From an engineering and styling design viewpoint, all 26 are fascinating, and, in their unique way, prime examples of the creative process known as 'design.'

Of course, nationality is no barrier to creativity, and contributions studied here come from America, Austria, France, Germany, Italy, and the UK.

MORGAN THREE-WHEELER

1911-1952 & 2011 on

ALTHOUGH ORIGINALLY A 'RUNABOUT,' THE MORGAN THREE-WHEELER'S SPORTING POTENTIAL WAS SOON RECOGNISED: THE LIVELY DEVICES COMPETING TO THIS DAY IN MANY FORMS OF MOTORSPORT.

THE TIME-TRAVELLING TRICYCLE

Stop me if I'm wrong, but there can't be any other vehicle, especially a three-wheeler, that began production before the First World War, and continued with the same basic design until after the Second World War, thus spanning the period 1911-1952. If that's not unusual enough, after a pause of some 60 years, to then resume production in 2011, receiving rave reviews from all and sundry, is really something. This could only occur if the vehicle possessed truly remarkable attributes recognised by the motoring public. So what makes Morgan three-wheelers so unique?

In the beginning

At the dawn of the twentieth century,

man's fascination with mechanical transport was barely past its springtime. Stephenson's *Rocket* was built in 1829, and the Wright brothers flew at Kitty Hawk in 1903.

In 1881 the Rev Prebendary Henry George Morgan begat a son: Henry Frederick Stanley Morgan (HFS). The good Reverend soon recognised his son's aptitude for all things mechanical, and managed, in 1901, to get him an engineering apprenticeship as a draughtsman at the Great Western Railway, Swindon. HFS worked for a short time in the drawing office, leaving in December 1904. The first vehicle he owned was an Eagle Tandem three-wheeler. Calling the aforementioned a strange contraption is being charitable: the driver sat high up over a driven, single rear wheel, while in front, between the wheels, was the passenger's wicker armchair. In the Eagle, HFS received a summons for exceeding the 12mph speed limit. However strange this bizarre contrivance, it set HFS on the path to his own famous three-wheelers which influenced Morgan design philosophy for over a century.

In 1905 this vicar's son set up a garage business with a friend, Leslie Bacon, at Malvern. The locals, in this rural community dominated by horse-drawn carriages, regarded cars as noisy, smelly things, with the clergyman's son's involvement adding insult to injury. Undeterred, our hero teamed up with another kindred spirit – the engineering master at Malvern College, Mr W Stephenson-Peach, a descendant of George Stephenson of Rocket fame. Together, they worked on HFS's creation – a three-wheeled cycle-car; a cross between a car and a motorcycle. Conventional cars of this period were described as 'horseless carriages,' their occupants sitting high up as in a horse-drawn vehicle, with little attempt to save weight, and using carriage technology such as wooden artillery wheels. (This type of wheel was responsible for the first UK motoring fatality, when one collapsed while descending Harrow Hill in North West London.)

Motorcycles had naturally inherited the lightweight, but strong, construction of bicycles, with their tube and lug frames and wire wheels, which Morgan adopted. Cycle-cars were not just a temporary aberration, but a valid form of transport; the only practical alternative being a sidecar outfit. HFS's 1909, single-seater Morgan prototype 'runabout,' registration CJ 743, was simplicity itself, displaying a philosophy of minimalism of which Colin Chapman of Lotus would have heartily approved. The novel design, now a two-seater, appeared at the 1911 Olympia Motor Cycle Show, and attracted backing from Richard Burbridge, MD of Knightsbridge store Harrods, enabling serious production to begin.

Construction

While Morgan's approach over the years was one of continuous improvement, the three-wheeler's mechanical layout remained essentially unchanged throughout its lifespan. Eschewing a motorcycle rear-end drivetrain, a motorcycle engine was positioned up front between the two front wheels, thus aiding stability and cooling. The propshaft went down the centre of a large diameter torque tube to a bevel box at the rear. This box had two output drive sprockets, with separate chains going to sprockets each side of the rear wheel, either of which could be selected by a dog clutch, giving a two-speed gear. This elementary transmission was successfully used from 1909 to 1930; in 1931 a more conventional three-speed gearbox was introduced, requiring only a single rear chain. Immediately behind the engine was a steel tube cruciform, bracing the top and bottom suspension outrigger tubes, and also locating the torque tube, plus two additional tubes running parallel to the torque tube helping to locate the bevel box. These latter tubes in the earliest models had silencer boxes at their front ends, the tubes doubling as exhaust pipes. The front wheel hubs were carried on an unusual sliding pillar incorporating bump and rebound springs, this system becoming a trademark Morgan feature which continued on the later four-wheelers. Early direct steering was by a tiller, which was soon replaced by a large steering wheel (geared steering didn't become standard until 1929).

The Austin 7 introduced in 1922 had front brakes, albeit via a handbrake, forcing Morgan to offer a front bowden cable system, which was also hand-operated. The Austin cost £165, Morgans started at £128, but, depending on who supplied the air- or water-cooled engines, could rise to £163, so the price gap between a 'real car' and this tricycle was diminishing. The issues of three-wheeler road tax, weight limit, reverse gear, and who could drive what on which license, still trouble three-wheelers to this day, often making questionable the running cost differential with four-wheelers.

However, certainly in the early1930s, if weighing under 8cwt (406.4kg) cycle-cars were taxed as motorcycles, at about half the cost of taxing a car – a significant saving over an Austin 7, which cost £7 annually, when average weekly wages were around £3.

The simple chassis design allowed many different motorcycle-type engines to be fitted, from single cylinder 500cc to 1100cc twins, with Matchless and JAP

V-twins being the usual fare. From 1933 to 1952 Ford car engines were also used, but on a more conventional chassis design.

Progress through competition

The vehicle's background and how it was engineered notwithstanding, it's hard to see why this Malvern tricycle attracted such a keen following over the years, but the reason is that it was always quick, and, eventually, very quick indeed.

The tranquil, cosy, 1900 world of Malvern, church, academia and the Great Western Railways witnessed the son of

an ecclesiastical family producing a tiny, three-wheeled runabout. Fast forward to 1988, when *Fast Lane* magazine reported the following: "August 1979, William (Bill) Tuer got his Morgan three-wheeler round Mallory Park racing circuit at an average speed of 93.8mph; August 1987, a Sierra RS Cosworth managed a lap record of 90mph […] After 25 laps of Mallory the venerable tricycle would lap the Sierra." The Morgan was also faster around Snetterton, with cornering ability its greatest advantage: surreal or what?

From day one, HFS realised he had to promote the reliability and performance of his brainchild against all the light cars, cycle-cars, motorcycles and sidecars available. Before the First World War and between the Wars, endurance trials and track racing became very popular. Events such as the Scottish Six Day Trial, the London-Exeter-London Trial, ACU (Auto Cycle Union) Six Day Trial, and similar events, attracted large crowds of knowledgeable enthusiasts. These trials were usually a series of extremely rough track hillclimbs over broken, often muddy surfaces all linked together by road sections, to provide an unforgiving test of man and machines. The good power-

GH 13

THE QUICKEST RACING MORGANS OFTEN EMPLOY TWO POSTWAR 500cc JAP SPEEDWAY BARRELS, RESULTING IN BOTH EXHAUST PIPES APPEARING ON THE SAME SIDE.

To Boldly Go

to-weight ratio of the Morgan proved a winner. Parallel to trials, circuit racing, such as at the famous Brooklands banked track, also allowed the Morgan to shine. Of course such a hotbed of competitive protagonists served as free engineering development, leading to a constant stream of upgrades and modifications honing this simple vehicle into an extremely sporting machine. Different engines were employed to tackle specific track records – 100mph was achieved in 1925 at Brooklands, and over 90mph maintained for an hour by Harold Beart's Blackburne-powered Morgan.

In 1924, EB Ware had a major accident at Brooklands, when his rear tyre tread became detached, and jammed one of the driving chains. The authorities subsequently banned Morgans from competing against four-wheelers (whose drivers were doubtless relieved to be rid of these irritatingly-fast rivals).

Non-believers will be converted by a ride in one of these unlikely machines, or by watching a classic motorcycle race. On the roads they are a joy; on the track spectacular: on fast bends the really quick ones are effectively cornering on two wheels as an unloaded front wheel just brushes the ground. Crouching behind the high scuttle, looking at, and hearing, an exposed V-Twin, and being aware of the suspension working as the air rushes past is an elemental experience.

Summary

There was always something derring-do and heroic about these vehicles. Several First World War Royal Flying Corps (RFC) fighter pilots used them, including Capt Albert Ball, VC, DSO, MC. One didn't have to look too hard to see a hint of the Sopwith Camel about the Morgan, and such high flying associations did their image no harm at all: the 'Aero' name tag first appearing in 1919 perhaps echoes this.

In a rational, ordered world, the arrival of the Austin 7 in 1922 should have sounded the death knell for the Morgan three-wheeler (as the 1959 Mini did for bubblecars), but this motoring aberration, which had never made a convincing four-seater, had a trump hand up its sleeve – it was fun, fast and frugal. As it re-emerged, blinking in the light in 2011 after a sixty-year hibernation, who could deny that this vicar's son had had a good idea ...

My life on wheels, Maurice Wiggin, Matters Morganatic:
"It was, in fact, very like a big cat in its ability to change in a moment from a purring, somnolent beast into a leaping, snarling fury." "The power unit, a big litre of highly-developed V-twin motor-bike engine, had bottom-end torque to a degree not merely unknown but practically unsuspected by the generality of road users.'

The Malvern trike (like its cousin the motorbike) has tended at times to attract, some would say, a regrettable type. Fond memories appeared in journals such as *Motor Sport*: "At the weekends me and my mate use to sit in a side turning off the Watford By-Pass, with the engine running, waiting for an SS Jaguar to go by ..."

"A demonstration in this water-cooled Matchless-powered example proved an assault on the senses. The exhaust barked in your ears, vision blurred by the elementary suspension is further confused by the agitated front wheels and mudguards. Exposed valve gear sends an oil mist rearwards. The previously mild owner now lost in his Biggles fantasy shouts 'She's good for eighty,' this gung-ho boast coincides with the brass radiator cap vibrating off and flying over our heads." (Author)

AUSTIN 7

1922-1939

ARCHETYPAL LATE 1950S/1960S MODIFIED 1934 AUSTIN 7 BOX SALOON. FRONT WINGS AND RUNNING BOARDS REMOVED. 15in (381mm) ALLOY WHEELS, BRIGHT PAINT, SUNROOF AND TUNING GOODIES PRE-EMPTING TODAY'S OPTION LISTS.

THE BOX SALOON – FAMILY TRANSPORT?

If those passing Cambridge University's Senate House early one morning in June 1958 had looked up, they would have been surprised to see a vintage Austin 7 sitting on the roof, 70ft (21.3m) above them. Likewise, in 1963 at St Johns, they would have seen a similar Austin 7 dangling under the Bridge of Sighs. These clever, illegal, dangerous and irresponsible student pranks were carried out under the cover of darkness. Interesting in themselves, the significance for our studies is the perpetrator's use of the then de rigueur little Austin.

Why a particular car endears itself to several generations of young people is debatable, but pertinent to this current examination of enthusiast fare. Why should this assembly of metal, rubber, cloth and glass – just like any other car – achieve a crossover into popular culture? The Austin 7, successful in its day, captured the imagination of an untapped market segment long after its production years were over. The Box Saloon, designed as 1920s/30s family transport, became the focus of a later generation, whose enthusiasm for performance modifications revealed what any soothsayer worth their goat entrails could see about what the future held in the form of hot hatches and sporty saloons.

Background to production Austin 7s

In 1921 the Austin Motor Company was on the verge of bankruptcy. Sir Herbert Austin wanted to provide motoring for the masses, but his board didn't regard a low-cost car as a solution. However, he was able, with the aid of draughtsman Stanley Edge, to design and build three prototypes. The Austin 7 was thus born in 1922, and proved a success with a public previously limited to a motorcycle or sidecar outfit. The earliest examples, such as the 1920s Chummy, remind one of a motorised Edwardian pram, but, with the price down to £165, the mass-market took to it, saving the company, and proving Sir Herbert right.

During its 17-year production run, model year changes and variations – from tourers, saloons, vans, doctor's coupés, and even supercharged sports cars – were almost too numerous to count. There were continuous improvements and upgrades to the mechanics and bodywork – up until 1930, the foot brake operated only on the rear wheels, and the handbrake on the front wheels, ie unconnected. But, through this myriad of change, the simple A-frame chassis and conventional 747cc, side-valve, water-cooled, four-cylinder engine were the bedrock that 7s were built on. The only fundamental modification was stretching the wheelbase by 6in (152mm) in 1931, allowing more rear passenger space. Proof of this little car's 'rightness' was the number built under licence by Rosengart (France), Dixi (BMW), and American Austin (Bantam), and also copied by Datsun. By the 1930s, an increasingly sophisticated market had turned the Chummy 'pram' into a well-proportioned family carriage, with it eventually morphing into the technically best, but rather over-bodied, 1935 Ruby model, which continued up to the end of production in 1939.

If Sir Alec Issigonis' 1959 Mini was probably the most significant vehicle in European motoring, Sir Herbert Austin's 1922 Austin 7 can claim its place in the family tree.

Sporting aspirations

Like so many successful car designs, regardless of modest origins, Austin 7s were used in all forms of competition from their earliest days. If 1931's 10.5bhp at 2400rpm (17 at 3800 by 1937), and a bit over 48mph* was standard top performance, the racing achievements of the 1920s and '30s – including six hours on Brooklands banked circuit averaging 83.41mph, were staggering, culminating in the 1935 twin-cam engines producing 116bhp at 7600rpm, and still just 747cc! Pre-empting John Cooper's 1960s Mini Coopers by over 30 years, Gordon England built factory-approved, lightweight, two-seater Austin 7s, with certificates guaranteeing 75mph.

Whilst the Austin was designed as family transport, the parallel sporting activity ensured that 'sports car' production variants blossomed. This resulted in a pretty, but fairly primitive, Sports Tourer two-seater costing £148, while a 'proper' four-seat Ruby saloon cost just £120; the 65, Nippy, Speedy and Ulster all exploited the profitable spin-off approach that would excite any brand manager today. Add the potent, well-publicised, one-off competition cars, and you have a sporty halo effect covering the whole Austin 7 image.

This potency is epitomised by the 1938 Issigonis Lightweight Special, which shone at the Prescott hillclimb in 1939: a single-seat, stressed alloy skin monocoque with rubber independent suspension, 80bhp supercharged Austin 7 engine, and weighing just 587lb (266kg). It's impossible to over-emphasise the Austin 7's place in motoring history. Sir Alec had previously hillclimbed an Austin 7

Ulster two-seater with a home-made split front axle, thus achieving independent front-suspension in the early 1930s.

What happened next

It was hardly surprising that, in the late 1940s and during the 1950s, with new cars costly and unavailable, hundreds of old, rather dilapidated Austin 7s were considered certainly better than nothing. The Austin 7's simple chassis attracted special builders like bees to honey, and converting family transport into two-seater sports cars became a national pastime for UK motoring enthusiasts. There was a thriving market for special bodies, such as those by Hamblin and Speedex, and tuning components to satisfy the demand for affordable sporty transport. The famous 750 Motor Club was founded in 1939 for modifying and racing these cars, and continues to this day; early participants included Colin

Chapman (Lotus), Jem Marsh (Speedex and Marcos), Keith Duckworth and Frank Costin (Cosworth), and numerous others.

But what was the appeal of modified Box Saloons in the 1950/60s?

A running theme with many mechanical objects, especially cars, that charm groups of enthusiasts is their combination of looks, character, and flaws – a bit like people. Everyone likes a game little trier, and the Austin 7 was surely that. Aesthetically, the 1933/4 Box Saloon is perfectly proportioned – its snub nose, upright windscreen and simple body look right. A box it certainly wasn't, however: the main body being subtly curved wherever you look. The large headlamps are the eyes of the car, and there is something of the faithful dog there. Painting the lower body in bright colours, lowering the suspension, wider wheels, etc, created in this observer a

MIKE FORREST'S EXTRAORDINARY CUT-AND-SHUT 1934 AUSTIN 7 BOX SALOON COMPETED IN 1960S 750MC CIRCUIT RACING, USING EVERY TRICK IN THE TUNER'S HANDBOOK.

desire to own. They are definitely cute, and, when suitably modified, project a timeless youthfulness. But an enthusiast does not need to explain or justify their enthusiasm: it just *is*.

The Forrest Saloon – an extreme example of Box appeal

Allan Staniforth, in his excellent *Race & Rally Car Source Book*, featured Mike Forrest's 750 Box Saloon of 1961. Mike, instead of throwing away the saloon body, as most special builders and 750 MC members did, got serious about making a true racer out of one. By the radical approach of cutting out horizontal slices amounting to 10in (250mm) from the superstructure and lower body, the frontal area was reduced by 20%, thus reducing aerodynamics drag and weight. Slicing the body and welding it all back together demonstrates the drive and determination the true believer can muster. No casual cut-and-shut job: Mike had experimented with cutting up pictures to ensure some aesthetic integrity. This operation pre-empted the equally demanding effort needed some years later to create the pretty 'sliced' Stewart and Arden Mini Sprints. Mike then employed every contemporary tuning tactic, plus several of his own.

All of this transformed the original saloon's apologetic, wheezing, 50mph to a 90mph contender, lining up on the grid with more conventional 750 MC racers. While Mike argued the purely rational case for this early example of the 'Silhouette Formula' – where competition cars have to bear at least a superficial resemblance to the production version – one likes to think he was essentially a fan of the charismatic little A7 Box.

As too, Henry Harris, still campaigning a Box Saloon, albeit supercharged, in a 1989 ten-lap handicap

750 MC race at Snetterton. Both Forrest and Harris justified their fully paid-up membership of the 'Box Boys' by using 15in (381mm) wheels, as opposed to the standard 19in (483mm). However, period nostalgia can only go so far: Harris was wearing a full-face helmet.

Testimony

My, perhaps perverse, interest in modified Austin 7 saloons began as soon as I was old enough to discover a world beyond aircraft. It was, specifically, the final iteration of the Austin 7 Box Saloon, the 1933/34 long-wheelbase that fascinated me. By the late 1950s and early 1960s, although their family transport days were over, the bright young things of the day loved them. Students and fellow travellers could pick them up cheaply, paint them bright colours, usually yellow or orange, whilst leaving the top in contrasting standard black, and generally have a hoot – I even saw a Tourer with a thatched roof!

Those with a little know-how and the necessary funds could, of course, use the tuning equipment intended for the builders of specials. This urge to create a sporty saloon was the starting point for all the hot hatches and countless option lists of today. Well-thumbed *Exchange and Mart* pages left one reeling; Bowdenex brake conversions – even Morris 8 hydraulics – independent front suspension, 15in (381mm) Speedex or Cambridge Engineering alloy wheels, flattened springs, twin-carburettors, alloy heads, lightened flywheels, competition clutches, close-ratio gears – the goodies were endless.

I visited a specialist in 1960s North London, whose business was devoted to the car. "It'll corner on rails," the louche proprietor claimed, leaning on a much-thrashed example with its complimentary oil drip. Engine implants were not unknown, and in the road outside sat

HENRY HARRIS' SUPERCHARGED AUSTIN 7 BOX SALOON WAS CAMPAIGNED IN THE LATE 1980S 750MC TRACK EVENTS, USUALLY INTIMIDATING KNEE-HIGH AUSTIN 7 SPECIALS.

an all-orange A7 Box, with front cycle mudguards replacing flowing wings and running boards, much lowered, and apparently 1172cc Ford E93A-powered. A mechanic in grease-stained overalls jumped in and raced off – quaint Chummy heritage a distant memory.

My favourite mental image of these sports saloons occurred early one 1960s Sunday morning in Central London, when I was going to see off the Brighton Veteran Car Run. In a now-classic Riley 1.5 we tried to hold station with a black-over-orange Austin 7 Box, along the traffic lights drag of the old Harrow Road. We finally gave the fired-up young blade and his lady best when he eventually ran a set of lights. I can still remember the fat rear tyres, puffs of smoke on the snatched gear changes, and fake Bonnie & Clyde bullet holes across his back window (period free gift with petrol). Stirring stuff.

1968, in the fitting environment of London's Central School of Art and Design car park, was the author's last sighting of this renegade breed.

OY 8166 was again a black-over-orange Box, sporting a 750 Motor Club

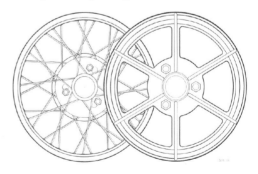

THE 1958 SPEEDEX ALLOY WHEEL DEMONSTRATES THE IMPACT OF THE AUSTIN 7 ENTHUSIAST. MANY USED 15in (381mm) WIRE WHEELS, BUT THE 2lb (0.9kg) LIGHTER ALLOY WHEEL WAS A REVELATION. PREVIOUSLY ONLY EXOTICA SUCH AS BUGATTI'S TYPE 35 HAD ALLOY WHEELS.

To Boldly Go

sticker, and crouching on 'Trials' wheels. The latter were the poor man's alloys, where four steel, channel-section spokes with large lightening holes were welded into the rim, replacing wire spokes. This was a last die-hard hooray, as postwar cars were available to the tuners, and Austin 7s were becoming worth more in their original state.

Conclusion

In today's product offer line-up, sporty cars make up a significant proportion, as does a strong aftermarket for performance equipment. Emerging from grim postwar austerity, people wanted a bit of fun.

In that early, green-shoots period, the Austin 7 Box demonstrated that sensible transport didn't have to be boring. For

PANDORA'S BOX WAS OPEN. THE AUSTIN 7 – THE CLARK KENT OF GENTEEL MOTORING SOBRIETY – WAS BEING TRANSFORMED INTO A TOUGHER ALTER EGO, REFLECTING MARKET DEMANDS STILL CURRENT TODAY.

the first time in the UK, enthusiasts, frustrated by lack of money and choice, seized the initiative and did their own thing, also pioneering the use of alloy wheels on road cars, foreseeing this now universally adopted enhancement by about 20 years. The original cars, teetering round on spindly 19in (483mm) wheels, could be transformed into personalised fun transport by lowering, widening, and pepping up the engine – what was not to like?

Automotive sociologists will note that, just as this specialised, but widespread, pursuit of sporting A7 saloons was in full bloom, the 1959 Mini was launched, and nothing would be quite the same again.

How the Austin 7 (a van version) arrived on the college roof in 1958 remained a mystery for 50 years until the culprits, now pillars of society, finally confessed. Using a large A-frame, steel rope and pulleys, they pulled up the vehicle to the roof parapet, reversed the angle of the A-frame, swinging the Austin through the frame and onto the roof's ridge. The Dean of Caius College, Rev Hugh Montefiore, guessed who the perpetrators were, but kept quiet and sent a crate of Champagne to their staircase. The local authorities took four days to bring down the illegally parked car.

The Austin 7 left hanging under the Bridge of Sighs was floated into position on four punts, then pulled up on ropes.

Ex-RAF pilot, Mike Forrest, trailered his slimline A7 Box racer behind a 20HP Rolls-Royce, created a city car, and later restored a Rolls-Royce Phantom.

OY 8166 belonged to art and design student Henry Harris. Early 1966 Henry had purchased a 'tired' 1932 Riley special from one David Jones, later morphing into David Bowie. The '60s really were a bit different ...

Authenticity is the watchword, but period modifications are sensibly accommodated; some high-performance Austin 7 engines even rely on modern Phoenix crankshafts and Renault 4 pistons, upsetting museum curators but not enthusiasts.

*To avoid any unpleasantness from true believers –
Motor's 17-11-31 road test of Long Wheelbase Box Saloon, 50mph.
Autocar's 6-11-36 road test of Ruby, 53mph.

G.H. 15

RALEIGH SAFETY SEVEN

1933-1936

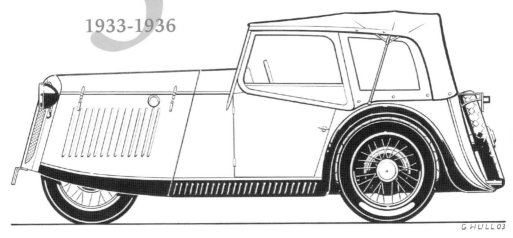

THE STANDARD 1933 RALEIGH SAFETY SEVEN SOFT TOP TOURER (ABOVE) WAS JOINED BY A COACH-BUILT SALOON (OPPOSITE), CLOSING THE GAP WITH ITS ARCH RIVAL, THE AUSTIN 7, EVEN FURTHER.

TOO GOOD TO BE FORGOTTEN

Mention 1930s three-wheelers, and enthusiasts will think Morgan or perhaps BSA – rather unfairly, Raleigh doesn't spring to mind. Reference sources usually mention the Nottingham tricycle, but only as the starting point for Reliant. The Raleigh, or Raleigh Safety Seven, although a well-engineered, successful design, is now a virtually forgotten curio.

Background

Three-wheelers tend to inhabit motoring no-man's land: they're not a member of the motorcycle fraternity, and are generally lampooned by the car world. Any credibility they do muster is won by sporting two-seater trikes that have their third wheel at the back, but then anyone

not stirred by a ride in an Aero Morgan or Grinnall Scorpion needs a check-up. Why, then, does the Raleigh merit attention, with its third wheel at the wrong end, and apparently little else going for it? It's because of schoolboy memories, a growing appreciation of design, and an old publicity booklet.

But first …

Raleigh Safety Seven versus Austin 7

The Austin 7 and the Raleigh, although different concepts, both attempted to fulfil the role of low-cost family motor. Surprisingly, the lighter three-wheeler was the larger of the two, longer by 16in (406mm), and with a 5in (127mm) wider track at 48in (1220mm). The Raleigh was happy cruising at 40-50mph, and, in 1935, *The Motor Cycle* achieved 58mph in it, which bettered the Austin.

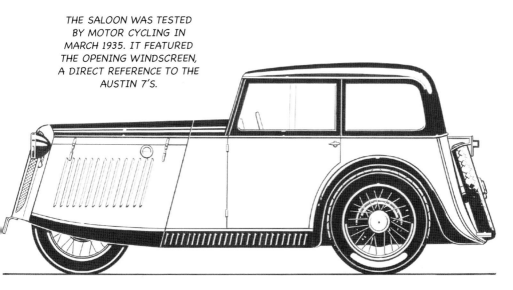

Surprisingly, the 1952 803cc Austin A30 had to settle for 62mph, albeit on low octane fuel. At 8cwt (406.4kg) the Raleigh was nearly 3cwt (152kg) lighter than a 1934 Austin 7 Box Saloon.

Most would assume the Austin 7's four wheels to be superior, but its handling and braking were not beyond criticism, and a back-to-back between the quad and trike might surprise. The Austin's swan song, the Ruby, produced similar bhp to the Raleigh, but weighed over 4cwt (203kg) more.

Mechanical and layout

So what stratagem did Raleigh designer TL Williams employ? To qualify for lower road tax, the weight could not exceed 8cwt (406kg), most of which was packaged as low as possible for stability. A substantial, under-slung chassis of two pressed beams ran forward from beneath the leaf-sprung rear axle, then swung up to a motorcycle-type steering head. Pressed forks were steered via worm and sector. A specially-designed Sturmey-Archer unit-construction engine and gearbox were tucked in behind the front wheel. This 742cc, air-cooled, side-valve, 80 degree V twin was mated to a three-speed and reverse non-synchromesh gearbox. Journals commented on the engine's robustness, with its large bearing surfaces and generous, 9-pint (5.1-litre) oil capacity. A wasted spark ignition system avoided a distributor.

Tuned to be a 'slogger' rather than for maximum performance, 17bhp was produced at 3000rpm, with enough torque to pull top gear down to 10mph, and achieving 50+mpg. The Raleigh engine/gearbox had three rubber mountings, and two silencer boxes for minimum vibration and noise. There was a propeller shaft to the axle.

Good braking was achieved by 10in (254mm) rear drums with a 7in (177mm) front, which discouraged the front wheel from locking first. The turning circle was a credible 21ft (6.4m). Three-track vehicles cannot avoid all road bumps, but the Raleigh's 18in (457mm) wheels helped iron them out.

There was little weight above the wheel centres, and the heavy, 6-volt battery was slung low beside the rear axle. 1933 press release information shows a scuttle-mounted fuel tank, which was later moved down behind the rear axle. This aided stability, but required an electric pump. Rear occupants sat over the rear axle; again, helping stability.

Body

The body was light and strong, with aluminium panels on a traditional ash frame. The general styling, topped off by hood and side screens, echoed contemporary tourers and sports cars, including a rear-mounted spare wheel. Cooling air for the engine was essential, hence the large, wire-mesh grille and body louvres. Front three-quarter view with the single wheel was unique, and not without a rakish charm. The centre-hinged bonnet with removable side panels allowed complete access to suspension and engine.

How the motoring press saw it

Period road tests can be misleading, and often laughably complimentary, with shortcomings barely hinted at. However, even reading between the lines, it's apparent that everyone liked the Raleigh. Aware of doubts over three-wheeler stability, testers were not shy to indulge in violent braking on lock, and drive fast round bends. These publications were, of course, also sampling powerful motorcycles, sidecar outfits, Morgans, and conventional cars. The Raleigh's flexible engine and excellent interior space were particularly noted. In June 1934 *The Motor Cycle* ended its test thus: "To sum up, the Raleigh handles like a car, provides the comfort of a well-sprung car, and has a really lively performance."

Given 1930 parameters, it's hard to see how the Raleigh could have been improved. Building on the company's

THE SECRET OF THE RALEIGH'S STABILITY WAS THE UNDER-SLUNG CHASSIS AND LOW-MOUNTED MECHANICAL COMPONENTS. COMPACT, CUSTOM-MADE, 742cc, V TWIN ENGINE AND LARGE REAR BRAKES ARE NOTABLE FEATURES. (AS RALEIGH BROCHURE)

experience with motorcycles and three-wheel commercials, Williams had got the Safety Seven right.

Sporting success

A period brochure from the owners' club sheds light on the Safety Seven's surprising competition successes. In the years between the wars, the popularity of Trials events made them the equivalent of today's rallying, with much emphasis on broken-surface hillclimbs linked by road sections. In 1934 Raleigh fielded a three-car works Trials team to demonstrate its three-wheeler's stability and performance.

The team was led by N Anderson and BFC Fallows of the company's Experimental Department. The people working there, having built the prototypes, and being involved in development work and testing, would have really understood the vehicle. Other team members were EN Adlington, a journalist, and RF Moore. Vehicles carried a passenger.

Before the 1934 Trial season, the team tackled a few hills, and decided to drop the axle ratio, lowering top gear from 5.1-1 to 6.5-1, and bottom from 16-1 to about 22.1. Adlington found bottom gear slow but "incredibly sure"; top speed on road sections was about 53mph. It pulled 5600rpm in second – "not bad for a slogger of a side-valve." He described staying on the tail of sports four-wheelers on tricky sections of the Lands End Trial. The Raleigh team drove overnight from Nottingham to Virginia Water "giving the vehicles a pretty severe thrashing."

The team entered major events, including London-Lands End, London-Edinburgh, and the Scottish Six Days Trial, and it was in these that Tom Williams' design had its glory days. Contemporary publications paint an evocative picture:

Motor Cycling:
"Barging over everything, cannoning off the banks, this extraordinary 750cc side-valve went up with utmost certainty." "Anderson's Raleigh three-wheeler suffered a lot of wheel spin, but clambered over everything like a great cat."

"The model did not turn over; it merely resumed an even keel and completed a perfect climb." "It was an impossible task for sidecars, which were rather overshadowed by Anderson's Raleigh." "Through the worst places it lurched with certainty, amid loud cheers from all the watching sidecar drivers whom it had so soundly beaten." "Everyone rose on tiptoe when the news spread – 'The Raleighs are coming!' These unorthodox machines swept up in procession: all fast, wonderfully steady, and totally devoid of crabbing."

The Light Car:
"For all this successful endeavour, Anderson was awarded a silver cup."

The Motor Cycle:
"Then came the most outstanding climb of the day, in the shape of N Anderson and the Raleigh Cyclecar, complete with hood." "One and all of the Competitors who had come down to watch the fun cheered it to the echo." "The Raleigh found no difficulty whatever – one might almost say as usual – and romped away with incredible acceleration that left the large crowd agape with astonishment."

The Raleigh triumphed over extremely hostile hills, out-performing solos and sidecars of up to 1100cc, all, like Morgans, handicapped by their single driven wheel. Considering the Safety Seven was a family tourer, it was a wonderful achievement – one of the three original team cars entered the 2004 Lands End Trial to mark the 70th

To Boldly Go

anniversary of the Raleigh's outstanding performance at this event.

The latter years

Having won its spurs, the Raleigh's time was to be brief. Produced throughout 1934 and 1935, changes in taxation began to hurt. Four-wheel road tax was reduced to £6 in January 1935, leaving three-wheelers at £4. Austin and Morris were bringing prices down to, and below, the Raleigh's £100. Acknowledging the battle with the Austin 7, Raleigh, at the 1934 Olympia Motorcycle Show, introduced a saloon version, even copying the Austin's opening windscreen.

Raleigh was a very experienced manufacturer, and would have been capable of producing significant numbers of Safety Sevens – some cite 3000. The London showrooms of Frank Waring Ltd, of Gt Portland St, were photographed, proudly full of shiny new examples, but one senses Raleigh's thoughts were elsewhere.

Due to changing markets, Raleigh decided to revert to its core business of bicycles. It had ceased making motorcycles in 1933, and, towards the end of 1935, all cars and vans. Some vehicles remained to be sold in 1936. TL Williams had left the company at the end of 1934, and, still keen on manufacturing three-wheelers, bought Raleigh stocks for his vans. It is believed that the letter 'R' on items such as foot pedals led him to choose the name Reliant.

Testimony

Our family's Raleigh Safety Seven was probably one of the last used as everyday transport. My father, an ex-sidecar man, was the sort of customer Thomas Lawrence Williams originally had in mind. A BSA M21 outfit had served well from the late 1930s, but, in the 1950s,

my mother rebelled against sharing a sidecar with two growing children, and in 1956 JD5266 allowed the family to at last sit together.

It's hard to imagine, but, even in the early 1960s, considerable numbers of prewar cars were in daily use. With not much money about, and pressure on manufacturers to export, anything with wheels was much sought-after. During our time with the Raleigh, a friend ran a 1950s Mark B Bond Minicar – basic, indeed.

Life is lived forward but only understood backward, and so it was with recollections of the Safety Seven, but it was obvious that my father liked it. He enjoyed accelerating round sharpish bends, exploiting the differential's indifference to turning left or right, unlike a sidecar outfit. With only a son as passenger, he indulged in full-throttle open bends, too, the Raleigh being low-slung and stable.

We kept the venerable device for several years of daily use, and occasional trips from NW London to the south coast. It nearly seized on a hot day on Dartmoor: a previous owner had added some very professional additional bonnet louvres, so I guess it was a known quirk.

It was a vehicle full of character. and referred to by the family as 'Sir Walter.' People who remembered the model in its heyday liked a chat; even hardened petrol pump attendants. It was a delight with the hood down and side-screens stowed. Its party piece was the starting-handle procedure, which, on freezing mornings, was inserted through the offside bonnet side-panel, much to onlookers' fascination.

OPPOSITE: 1934 TRIAL SPECTATORS AND FELLOW COMPETITORS WERE SURPRISED AND IMPRESSED BY THE THREE-STRONG RALEIGH SAFETY SEVEN WORKS TEAM. STABILITY, TRACTION, AND A WILLING ENGINE GRANTED THIS FAMILY TRANSPORT MUCH SUCCESS.

G.H.14

JD5266, 'SIR WALTER,' THE FAMILY'S 1950S/EARLY 1960S DAILY TRANSPORT, WITH ADDITIONAL BONNET LOUVRES AND WIDER WINDSCREEN PILLARS. IT DEMONSTRATED TYPICAL 1930 SPORTS-TOURER STYLING; MINUS ONE FRONT WHEEL.

JD5266 had obviously been owned previously by an enthusiast, as, apart from extra bonnet louvres, there was evidence of a non-standard fan rig. The windscreen frame had been stiffened with wider pillars, and the wiper mechanism moved to the top. No doubt the motorcycle/car hybrid's charm attracted tinkerers.

Summary

Design solutions for low-cost family transport invariably fascinate. The sidecars, Morgans, Austin 7s, and so on, helped get the country mobile. The Raleigh Safety Seven deserves to be remembered as a 'wrong way round' three-wheeler that seated four, and actually worked rather well.

We saw a much modified example with an Austin 7 engine tidily installed, which is what Williams did when he produced his Reliant three-wheel vans; even manufacturing his own version of the Austin engine.

Motorcycle journalist Cyril Quantrill reminisced in *Classic Motor Cycle*, in 1990, about 'Ulsterbarrow': a certain EG Smith had fitted an Austin Ulster engine into a Safety Seven (these were available supercharged!). Cyril commented: "Very prone to lifting the inner wheel on fast curves but enormous fun: I returned it quite reluctantly."

An added piquancy to the Raleigh v Austin contest is that at least one Austin 7 type special used the Raleigh V-twin.

A Safety Seven *would* have won the Scottish Six Day Trial but was penalised for minor body cracks – Trials were never a stroll in the park.

WILLYS JEEP MB & FORD GPW

1941-1945

THE UBIQUITOUS 1941 JEEP WAS EMPLOYED IN MANY MILITARY ROLES. THIS LONG-RANGE DESERT GROUP EXAMPLE IS PRACTICALLY DISAPPEARING BENEATH ADDITIONAL EQUIPMENT.

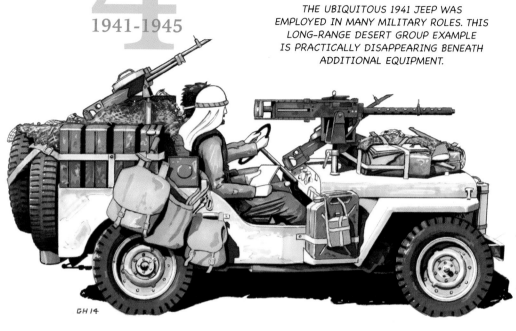

GH 14

'LIKE AN OLD FRIEND'

For a certain generation the World War Two Jeep was as helpful and reliable as a good friend. With hindsight it became something of a symbol of hope for an eventual victory, because after several desperate years of isolation for Britain, the Americans joined in. One never forgot its origins, as all were left-hand drive. It was built at Willys and Ford plants in America, where approximately 640,000 examples were produced.

Background

Due to increasing international tension in the 1930s, the American military decided it wanted a general-purpose vehicle to replace its motorcycles and sidecar outfits. The German army had come to the same conclusion; hence its VW Beetle-based

Kübelwagen. In typical bureaucratic style, the US powers-that-be, after a period of rumination, wanted prototypes submitted, and 70 test vehicles in four months! Despite this unreasonable time-frame, the final result was pretty well perfect. This, to some extent, seemed due to the two submissions from the American Bantam car company and Willys-Overland Motors being melded together. In production from 1941 to 1945, such was demand that the Ford Motor Company had to be employed as a mass producer.

The initial design brief was for a rapid deployment reconnaissance and communications vehicle, which could, at a pinch, be manhandled by a small group of soldiers. However, the design proved so adaptable that it became a ubiquitous presence in all theatres of war, and fulfilled many roles. It was nippy enough for scouting ahead, but had sufficient power to act as a tractor, pulling various artillery pieces, trailers, and mounted heavy machine guns, and carrying several stretchers as a field ambulance.

Mechanicals

In essence, the design couldn't have been much more basic, and, in modern parlance, an exercise in minimalism. Everything was well proven and virtually unbreakable.

The chassis was straight out of the 'Detroit iron' handbook: two pressed steel longerons ran from front to back, with cross members forming a 'ladder.' The engine was a conventional, torquey, 2199cc, side-valve unit, producing 54bhp of 'grunt' at 4000rpm. Both solid axles had differentials and drive shafts to supply four-wheel-drive, powered from an offset transfer-box at the back of the engine. Longitudinal leaf springs were used front and back.

Surprisingly for an American solution, dimensions were laudably restrained at 131in (3327mm) long by 62in (1575mm) wide. The large diameter wheels and knobbly tyres immediately caught the eye. A relatively short-wheelbase of 80in (2032mm) and good ground clearance meant its minimal nose and tail overhangs didn't easily foul when tackling rough ground. Again, to avoid grounding, the exhaust system was tucked up high, with the silencer in front of the rear wheel.

Body

The Jeep's open 'punt' body carried four occupants sitting on rather than in it. There was virtually no superstructure above the bonnet line, apart from a windscreen that could fold flat on hinges. All Jeeps had a folding canvas hood, and the capacity to fit side-screens. Although often seen in combat situations with windscreens folded down onto the

bonnet, and no weather protection in practice when used as support vehicles on airfields, etc, their canvas hoods were usually in evidence, especially in a usually-wet UK.

When operating in the field with no direct support, the Jeep generally carried jerrycans of petrol alongside the rear-mounted spare wheel; spades and axes were also pretty much standard equipment. In the desert, the vehicle all but disappeared beneath numerous jerrycans, extra spare wheels, supplies for extended patrols, and camouflage netting.

For some special deployments, such as ambulances, small numbers of Jeeps were fitted with conventional coach-built bodies, but the usual kerb weight for the Jeep was just 2293lb (1040kg).

The 'flying' Jeep

The inevitable stalemate of the First World War's trench warfare had prompted the German army, 20 years later, to use the Blitzkrieg tactic of rapid deployment of highly mobile armour and parachute/glider troops. The Allies responded with their own similar airborne forces, including parachute and glider divisions. Such was the Jeep's general purpose nature, relatively light weight and compact proportions, that it was regarded as an essential component by the newly-formed airborne forces. This led to perhaps its most interesting and glamorous phase.

Deploying a vehicle like the Jeep deep behind enemy lines would obviously be extremely advantageous for rapid ground movement. But how to get it there? The obvious answer might appear to be by parachute, but this was easier said than done, because, apart from needing a bomber to carry it slung underneath, and complicated clusters of parachutes, the Jeep could, when released, drift away from its parachuting crew before touchdown. Trying to deliver it accurately tended to involve lower and lower drops with fewer and smaller parachutes. Jeeps were considered tough enough to survive being dead-dropped from around 10ft (3.05m) but one, possibly apocryphal, account tells of the parachutists climbing into their Jeep after it had touched down but failing to get it to start. Flinging open the bonnet they found that the impact had caused the engine mounts to shear, and the engine was buried in the ground!

Another 'flying Jeep' was the Hafner Rotabuggy, named after its inventor, Raoul Hafner. Essentially, an autogyro structure was built around a Jeep, and when towed behind, typically, an Armstrong Whitworth Whitley tug aircraft, the rotors auto-rotated, enabling it to fly. Some very brave men actually got this unlikely device to work, but the whole contraption was obviously marginal, and the Jeep had to shed all the 'aircraft' components – probably under fire – before it could be used. But, again, this demonstrates just how badly the military wanted the Jeep as a part of its attack force.

The solution eventually employed, in significant number, was to load the Jeep, complete with trailer and guns, etc, into the large Horsa assault glider. The first Jeep arrived in England in November 1941; two days later it was having a fitting for the early Horsa mock-up, such was the need to equip airborne forces to answer the opposition's Blitzkrieg warfare. (The American Waco glider was also extensively used, but could carry one Jeep only.)

GH14

THE FIRST JEEP IN THE UK WAS IMMEDIATELY COMMANDEERED TO ENSURE IT WOULD FIT INTO THE HORSA ASSAULT GLIDER. GOOD FOR TOWING GUNS, TRAILERS, RECONNAISSANCE, CARRYING STRETCHERS, ETC, IT CHANGED BATTLEFIELD TACTICS OVERNIGHT.

To Boldly Go

This led to the now most collectable and sought-after 'Airborne Jeep.' The vehicle was driven and manhandled up a ramp, in through the Horsa's wide side door, and turned ninety degrees into the fuselage. To gain clearance, much of the front bumper was sawn off, and a quick-release steering wheel was used to clear the Horsa wing's box spar running through the fuselage. Windscreens were left behind, and even items such as grab handles were jettisoned to save weight. On landing, explosive bolts blew off the Horsa's tail, allowing the Jeep to exit out the back – no points for forgetting to reattach the steering wheel in the heat of the moment!

Later Horsas had a nose that hinged upward, like the Waco, to aid ingress and egress. By these tactics the Jeep, crew and payload could be delivered accurately, and in large number, into very precise landing zones.

The Airborne Jeeps were role-specific: armed reconnaissance, towing anti-tank guns or trailers, stretcher racks for field ambulance, radio communication – all special roles where speed and surprise were everything, ably demonstrating this newcomer's versatility in the battlefield.

In retrospect
The Jeep is a perfect example of form following function, and purity of design. There isn't an ounce of fat on it; it's a tough, lean machine, perfect for its time and situation. Over the decades, amongst the ranks of automotive exotica, the Jeep's status is well acknowledged, and it often appears in design list Top Tens. Not bad for a vehicle that, in military speak, was often described as a 'quarter-ton truck.'

A Horsa assault glider on exercise snapped its tow line to the multi-engined tug aircraft. Being a hot day with plenty of thermal air currents, the glider pilot decided to attempt to reach an American bomber airfield. Just making it, the Horsa landed right on the edge of the vast expanse of concrete. After a while, a Jeep with a big board on the back roared up, circled round the glider and roared off again, which it did a couple of times. Written on the Jeep's board were the words 'FOLLOW ME' ... well, so I've been told anyway.

Airborne Jeep drivers in combat zones often removed the distributor rotor-arm if leaving their Jeep, because both sides tended to 'borrow' these handy vehicles. An anti-tank gun crew lost its Jeep to a Chaplain when he drove off, unaware he was taking the spare ammunition with him.

When in the army, Elvis Presley spent hours 'sandpapering' the exhaust on his unit's Jeep until it shone. At the inspection his officer said "Son, that is the sharpest exhaust I've ever seen on a Jeep." Rock and Roll ...

CITROËN 2CV & DYANE

1948-1990

THE CITROËN 2CV (DEUX CHEVAUX) WAS AN UGLY DUCKLING THAT EXACTLY FULFILLED ITS RUSTIC DESIGN BRIEF. THE DYANE DID EVERYTHING BETTER … AND DIDN'T FRIGHTEN THE HORSES, EITHER.

BODY LANGUAGE – A QUESTION OF STYLE?

A good case can be made for including psychologists in car design teams – not, as you might think, to study designers, but rather the subliminal impact of the shapes they create. Across vehicles there is little technical difference between makes; therefore, emotional perceptions of a design hold sway as never before. A car's body language is critical, but this factor is barely understood. Insight into this elusive aspect of why one vehicle is preferred over another can be gleaned from the strange case of the Citroën 2CV. If the 1955 DS is Citroën's Goddess, the 2CV is its gardener, complete with trousers held up by string. The Deux Chevaux is a case study in

its own right, but what should also engage us here is its alter-ego, the Citroën Dyane, the 2CV's superior, more refined replacement. However, while the 2CV has entered the Classic Car Hall of Fame, its urbane, younger sibling has been wheeled off into obscurity.

Background

Citroën recognised in the 1930s that a large percentage of France's population were low-paid farm workers, often using horse transport in rustic localities. They couldn't afford the cars available, which probably wouldn't have been suitable, anyway. With admirable insight, Citroën set about designing a car for this 'hostile environment.' Lightweight, small, and economical, with an easy-to-maintain engine, and suspension able to cope with very rough tracks and even ploughed fields, the resultant Deux Chevaux was a masterpiece of minimalism, never surpassed.

The Second World War disrupted production plans, and prototypes had to be squirrelled away. By 1948, Citroën had further 'refined' its 'farm worker' car, and revealed it to the world. Just over half a century later 8.7 million 2CVs and variants had been sold.

2CV chassis and mechanicals

The heart of a 2CV is a simple chassis, consisting of two pressed-steel longerons running bumper to bumper, the middle part of which is boxed in, forming the floor of the passenger compartment, and a torsionally stiff mounting platform for the leading and trailing suspension arms. Mid-point on this chassis box is one horizontal spring each side. The suspension arms have a rod pressing against the spring, thereby interconnecting front and rear wheels to deal with bumps; ie, as the front wheel is pushed up it forces the rear wheel down. Alex Moulton did the same thing 14 years later with hydraulics on the hydrolastic Austin 1100.)

Forward of the chassis box sits the front-wheel drive engine and gearbox, whilst behind the chassis box is the fuel tank. The front has inboard brakes on the differential output shafts (drums later replaced by discs); the rear has conventional hub-mounted brakes.

The engine is an alloy air-cooled, four-stroke flat twin, which began life as 373cc, evolving to 425cc, and finally 602cc. It is extremely easy to maintain, as there is no distributor, just a wasted spark, and no head gaskets. The gearbox can be regarded as a three-speed with a very high fourth top gear.

The chassis is a strong, light, original solution to the demanding design brief.

2CV body

As the chassis is structurally self-contained, the body only has to support itself, and is not required to resist torsional or bending loads like a monocoque. There was very little attempt to put any strengthening pressed shape into panels, apart from corrugations on the large bonnet.

Bonnet, doors and boot lid are located by a full-length rolled hinge, allowing them to be lifted off. The roof is canvas, and originally extended right down to the rear bumper. The body is bolted to chassis outriggers.

To save weight, glass areas are small, and only later 2CVs had a glass panel in the rear quarter. The superstructure is best described as lightweight: the car weighs 1300lb (600kg), and, at 152in (3.86m) long, is not particularly small.

For maintenance purposes the front wings are attached via large, visible nuts, enabling rapid removal, and, with the bonnet removed, the oily bits are totally exposed to the tender mercy of any adjustable spanner-wielding farmer.

The seats are reminiscent of village hall steel-tube stacking chairs, but, with the fabric seat and back suspended by numerous rubber bands, simple and comfortable. All seats can be removed for picnics or carrying anything other than people.

How the Dyane differs from the 2CV

Motoring enthusiasts can generally be divided into those who have driven 2CVs and 'get' the car, and those who haven't and don't.

A further division exists, however: Dyane owners who believe that this was possibly the best light car ever. Given the rustic 2CV's success, it was sensible to upgrade the vehicle for the growing aspirations of a more sophisticated market.

Imagine, if you will, the Tin Snail being driven into a 'Molecular Improvement Facility,' the controls set for 'Improve Product by 25%,' and the resultant Dyane driven out. *Car Magazine,* in 1973, was beguiled and bemused by its general ability, and smooth, flat twin's eventual terminal velocity, when driven flat-out.

Whatever the 2CV did right, its young sibling bettered. Whereas the early 2CV had a canvas flap over its boot (later a metal lid), the Dyane had a proper early hatchback. The older car's tiny windscreen gave tall drivers, curious about the view ahead, a stoop, so its replacement sported a splendidly enlarged screen. The new kid on the block also had a remote fresh-air intake, replacing the original's opening flap – which, in fairness, had a wire-mesh screen to sift luckless insects.

The side windows on the eccentric 2CV hinged up to fix into rubber bungs, or could be left to flap in the wind. Following a 2CV with both front windows unsecured is reminiscent of an Aardman Animation plasticine chicken attempting take-off. Not without Gallic charm, these windows could, however, give the unaware a playful crack on the elbow. Needless to say, the Dyane's windows moved as effortlessly as those on Issigonis' early Mini.

Although both bodyshells were lightweight, in comparison, the older car's verges on flimsy, and, often, in gusting wind or the wake of a lorry, the sky could be seen through gaps at the top of the door as it was sucked outward. The 2CV's bonnet was so flexible that its sound-deadening pad, seemingly made from re-cycled French army blankets, actually stiffened it. This wobbly bonnet was held open by a long stick: the posh Dyane employed a telescopic tent-pole.

Whilst, over the years, the 2CV's body lost its corrugations, they seemed to remain in spirit; the 'Anderson Shelter' van versions always stayed true to the 1930s Junkers Ju52 aircraft that inspired it.

Styling 'aesthetics'

Apparently, styling of the Deux Chevaux was influenced by the great Flaminio Bertoni, of Citroën Light 15 and DS fame. However, legend has it that the engineers kept him at arm's length, to avoid interfering with their puritanical pursuit of functionality. One struggles to describe the resulting style. Unusual in its ability not to look 'right' from any angle, there is still the undeniable appeal of an ugly duckling, the body having the tail-in-the-air stance of a mallard nibbling pondweed. In addition, the wheels can appear semi-detached.

The styling background of the Dyane is a little confused. When Citroën scooped up Panhard in 1964, the latter's aerodynamicist and designer, Louis Bionier, became involved, but it seems that Citroën's Robert Opron's design team was also influential. If a style is successful, parentage is quickly claimed, but, sadly, the Dyane remains something of an orphan.

Panhard built the prototype, and certainly the new body sitting on the 2CV's platform was a cleaner, less bitty offering. The unorthodox, hollowed-flanks were intended to stiffen the thin metal panels, and came from Bionier's superb Panhard 24CT. A school of thought suggests that the Dyane was going to be marketed as a 'Panhard 2CV' – after all, the name Dyane is close to Dyna, a well-known Panhard model in France ...

On the road

I'm a fan of both the original 2CV and its dynasty – they're practical, and a hoot to boot. The driving technique is energy conservation and maintaining momentum

at any price. The cars are virtually impossible to overturn, despite heroic roll-angles when cornering. Early 2CVs strained their way to 55mph; later ones achieving the aerodynamic facts of life at 69mph.

The Dyane inherited the French philosophy of allowing cars to achieve terminal velocity on the country's long, straight, tree-lined roads. I've often loped along on motorways in a Dyane at speeds the police only just tolerate. In a colleague's Fiat coupé we paced a Dyane that was holding well over 80mph. Its fabric roof had sprung the side pop-studs, and was sucked up into an Arc de Triomphe. This simple, if accidental, application of variable-geometry-

A GOOD CASE CAN BE MADE FOR THE VERSATILE CITROËN DYANE BEING THE ULTIMATE LIGHT CAR. THE 602cc ENGINE COULD, GIVEN TIME, ACHIEVE SURPRISINGLY HIGH CRUISING SPEEDS.

G H 14

could emerge functioning normally, but, whilst I am a fan, the same cannot be claimed of the BMC Mini.

Despite superior performance, the Dyane's fuel economy was as good as the frugal 2CV; it had the same super-comfortable ride, was quieter, and had disc brakes first. No one could argue against the Dyane being the better car. Given that the 2CV's raison d'être was functionality, even here, it had to bow to the upstart. The most fanatical Deux Chevaux helmsman had to acknowledge that a legendary car had been greatly improved, with no downside.

History's verdict

Despite the Dyane's evolutionary superiority, Darwin would have been dismayed to learn what happened next. People were willing to go to extreme lengths to keep their 2CVs on the road, while Dyanes approached Dodo status. The peasant's motorised tin-shed is an icon, albeit an odd one, and the 'svelte' Dyane isn't. The 2CV's popularity isn't just a recent trend: its production outlived (1948-1990) the Dyane (1967-1983). In France the Renault 4 took over from the 2CV, and the Dyane lost out.

Anyone who enjoys motoring (which 2CV drivers clearly do), and doesn't care what others think (which 2CV drivers clearly don't), should, in theory, have chosen the Dyane. The fact that they didn't and haven't speaks volumes about the emotive aspects of car appeal. The 2CV is an example of visual charisma outweighing the merits of a superior offering. Many people simply like the

aerodynamics was obviously effective. No doubt the low nose, flat underside, and high tail also extracted the most out of the miserly 602cc.

The same 32bhp Dyane remained stubbornly UK legal when fully-laden, with its tail forced down, and its nose drag-inducingly high. The driver of a Dyane, after a 'press-on' motorway drive,

To Boldly Go

2CV's body language, which could cause design experts to pause, considering how quirky that communication is.

Look at some of the other humble vehicles that refuse to die, or are born-again: the Morris Minor, Fiat 500, VW Beetle, and Mini. Such is their visual potency that TV adverts and programmes often use them to set a scene. All aimed at minimal motoring, they were not shy of employing novel design and engineering. These modest devices got people involved and feeling protective towards them. Product Planners and Brand Managers intone "Must appeal to younger buyers" – ironically, the cars mentioned have appealed across the generations, regardless of class, age, or gender, all without owner-profiling, clinics, focus groups, and so forth. My sister, for instance, had no interest in cars other than her 2CV.

Cars are getting better and better, but 2CVs continue to be resuscitated, outliving subsequent superminis such as the Mini Metro.

Conclusion

Considering the commercial burden that car programmes carry, their subconscious appeal is still not properly understood. Designers can tend towards montages of visual elements, which may or may not appeal. Many styling cues are influenced by predators: mean eyes, big mouths, and bulging haunches, which may suit some, but not all – you only need so much implied aggression in a Tesco car park.

It's a truism that ugly cars don't sell, but charismatic cars may, and the gauche 2CV appears to be a classic example of this. There is more to this than meets the eye … Psychologists could sort it out, and give designers a reference manual on what appeals to whom and why.

In the meantime, when next you see a Citroën 2CV, reflect and ponder on this unlikely survivor …

The first UK 2CVs were built at Slough. They had 'suicide' front doors, ie rear-hinged. I was getting a lift to school when a front door came open at about 40mph. The door flew back with great velocity, striking the rear door, the rubber check-strap responded with equal fury and hurled the door back again, closing it. The noise inside the car was like someone firing both barrels of a 12-bore shotgun in rapid succession.

Two Frenchmen driving a 2CV round the world lost all engine oil in the Atacama desert in Chile. The washboard surface had vibrated off the oil cap. A passing local forced some bananas down the oil filler enabling the engine to continue propelling the vehicle.

For the 1981 James Bond film *For Your Eyes Only*, a yellow 2CV was fitted with a 1100cc Citroën GS four-cylinder engine and anti-roll bars, but the director demanded the latter were removed …

LJK Setright –
"The most intelligent application of minimalism ever to succeed as a car." "Remorseless rationality."

Pub quiz question –
What was the last new car sold in the UK to have a starting handle?

BOND MINICAR
1949-1966

THE 1949 MKA BOND MINICAR WAS NOVEL AND CUTE. REFLECTING POSTWAR AUSTERITY, WITH CONVENTIONAL CARS NOT BEING READILY OBTAINABLE, THE APPARENTLY UNLIKELY, 122cc-POWERED DEVICE FULFILLED A NEED.

THE MECHANISED PONY AND TRAP

In the annals of motorised marginal transport, one is spoilt for choice when attempting to select a champion from winged-wheel bicycles, through motorised rickshaws, to the Citroën 2CV. Man has demonstrated limitless imagination in transporting himself with what often appears to be less than the minimum power required, but, to this observer, the Bond Mk A Minicar is right up there: half-car, half-not much at all.

Background

Interesting vehicles always have interesting individuals somewhere in the vicinity; in this case it's Lawrence Bond – a somewhat driven engineer. After an engineering apprenticeship, Lawrence worked at the Blackburn Aircraft Company, which, no doubt, influenced his later weight-saving use of aluminium sheet and castings, perspex, fibreglass, and a generally minimalistic approach. As well as the Minicar, he designed 500cc racing cars, the successful (and pretty) Berkeley three- and four-wheelers, scooters, small boats and camping

To Boldly Go

trailers, all demonstrating innovation and lightness. The Bond works was at Preston, in Lancashire.

Method of execution ...

This original Bond three-wheeler of 1949 has been compared to a pony and trap, the two occupants sitting low behind a mechanical 'horse' – the nag in question being a single, steerable, 8in (203mm) wheel, cantilevered off of a cast-aluminium bulkhead plate; the wheel, in turn, having a 122cc Villiers two-stroke engine producing 5bhp at 4400rpm, and three-speed gearbox cantilevered off it. So, the diminutive power unit, driving the front wheel via an exposed chain, swung around with the front wheel.

Claims of the Mk A achieving 100mpg were probably not too fanciful – assuming the vehicle could cover a hundred miles. These early Bonds had no reverse gear, necessitating only a motorcycle licence to drive them.

The driver influenced the direction of the front wheel by means of cable and bobbin steering (don't ask). The loads were obviously high, requiring a large steering wheel, and broken cables were not unknown before basic rack and pinion steering – and later worm and sector – were employed, mercifully. The weight of the overhung engine tended to turn its wheel to the left if the road was heavily cambered, and drivers began, no doubt, to develop the asymmetric muscles of medieval longbow archers. The muscles of early owners also got a workout, pulling an under-dash starter cable attached to the carry over kickstart of the motorcycle engine; failing that, one opened the bonnet, straddled the machine, and used the kickstart directly (try not to dwell on that image).

The two rear wheels were unsprung, but did at least have cable brakes ... unlike the front wheel, which, although

lacking a brake, boasted a road spring! All components were attached to the aluminium monocoque chassis/body. There was a plexiglass windscreen, which didn't resist too well the abrasive attention of the manual windscreen

THE BOND'S 'MECHANICAL HORSE' GREW FROM A VILLIERS 122cc VIA 197cc (AS SHOWN), TO – FINALLY – THE 1966 250cc TWIN. THE PRESTON-BUILT BOND SURVIVED FOR 17 YEARS BECAUSE IT WORKED QUITE WELL.

wiper. A canvas hood supplemented creature comforts, the pampered occupants being further cosseted by a padded bench seat.

The entire contrivance weighed merely 310lb (140kg), and if there is a simpler vehicle answering to the name of car, it's hard to imagine what it is. Aesthetically, the front looked like a fairground dodgem, and the back, well, just a back with a number plate and one minuscule tail-lamp.

G.H. 14

To Boldly Go

Amazingly, this vestigial carriage was successful enough to encourage upgrades. In 1951 the Mk B appeared with a 197cc engine (boosting top speed from a desperate 43mph to a bold 50mph), plus rear suspension and a safety glass windscreen. Rear bodywork was extended to include rudimentary, and ambitiously-named, rear 'seats,' or for carrying luggage, and there was even a spare wheel.

Surprisingly, for such an inventive chap, Lawrence's Mk A and Mk B Bonds didn't exploit the Minicar's famous potential party piece: an ability to turn within its own length. In 1953, the Mk C arrived, with cavernous, bolted-on front wings that allowed the overhung power unit to swing 90 degrees both ways: like a dog chasing his tail, or a Whirling Dervish, it could spin round on the spot. Later, Bonds would have a dynastart, allowing the engine to run backwards, enabling the vehicle to chase its tail in reverse for added entertainment. The Mk C also had rubber-in-torsion rear suspension, and a front brake to help tame the beast.

In the event

Despite the original Minicar's specification, or, indeed, lack of it, the little car did its job. Relentless improvements created Mks A, B, C, D, E, F, and G, with 1966 being the final year, and, all told, some 26,500 examples were produced.

Bearing in mind that Lawrence Bond built the prototype in 1948 to use as his wife's shopping car, as the marque progressed, some owners actually enjoyed very long journeys in a Bond. As a promotional stunt in 1954, a Mk C was an unofficial entrant in the famous Monte Carlo Rally, completing the course, and then driving back to the UK. Other such epic journeys, such as 1960's London-Paris-Brussels-London (524 miles) in 14 hours running time, all received good media coverage. And many period yarns exist of Bonds loaded to the gunwales with people and camping gear, cheerfully venturing forth on high-mileage holidays.

Idiosyncratic vehicles often generate a degree of enthusiasm, and even affection, from their protective custodians, with any shortcomings apparently adding to the appeal, and even adventure. A large owners' club was formed, for example, with a magazine offering handy tips, such as making a shelf for your Thermos flask and sandwiches. These like-minded folk also got together for quite vigorous time trials, etc, usually against each other, of course.

A place in history

The popularity of the Mk A Bond Minicar is a potent indication of how limited the motoring scene was in postwar Britain. In the late 1940s, the country was financially drained, and steel was only available for those with export licences. Family transport was effectively limited to prewar cars, motorcycles and sidecars. Anyone who experienced a 1930s, ill-maintained (pre-MOT) Austin or Ford, etc, would have regarded a shiny new Bond in a more favourable light than the spoilt-for-choice motorist of later decades. In addition, the then new Morris Minor cost twice as much as Preston's tricycle.

This Minicar is an unusual case of an automotive evolutionary blind alley. The social and economical circumstances of 1949 created an unlikely, but surprisingly viable, vehicle. This strange bird managed to cling to its precarious perch for 17 years, trying to adapt to survive and evolve; even growing new plumage in an effort to attract customers. The final iteration, the Mk G, had a Villiers twin engine of 250cc producing 14.6bhp at 5500rpm, almost 60mph, and an average 58mpg within reach. But, despite 10in (255mm) wheels like the 1959 Mini, a reverse-rake back window like the 1959 Ford Anglia, hydraulic brakes like the 1931 Morris Family Eight, and four seats, the Bond Minicar still had to rely on its Mk A swinging engine inheritance.

By 1966 the new breed of conventional cars from the 1950s were within 'previously-owned' financial reach, and, of course, also the game-changing Issigonis Mini. The Bond Minicar went the way of the Dodo, as an increasingly sophisticated market moved on. This Bond was a child of its time: needs must when the devil drives, and this devil's name was austerity. But, as is so often the case, this peculiar and awkward bird had the last laugh, as surviving examples are cherished and highly collectable.

The Bond's engine and gearbox was so easily removed that at least one owner, faced with a Minicar refusing to start, opened the bonnet to find the power plant had been stolen!

Another time, when a Bond refused to proceed, the owner stoically unbolted the engine, put it in a sack, hefted it over his shoulder, and walked to the nearest garage to get a sheared Woodruff key replaced.

A line from *The Light Car* magazine:
"A sharp protuberance on the rear door pillar [this Mk C had a door on the passenger side only] will, we hope, be eliminated. It can catch clothing with a quite devastatory effect."

June 1960, *The Bond Magazine*:
"Bond Minicar owners find it irritating to have to lift the bonnet to turn the petrol on or off. This can be overcome by the use of a small diameter rod: you may be able to raid your son's Meccano outfit and find a very suitable rod and other parts." Drawing supplied.

Coda:
Nothing, if not adventurous, Bond introduced the Minicar's successor in 1965. The 875 was a four-seater that married a Hillman Imp rear end to a single front wheel. John Surtees, in the prototype, achieved 100mph at Brands Hatch – the engine was de-tuned shortly afterwards.

CITROËN 2CV PICK-UP
1953-1961

SURPRISINGLY, THIS 'TYPICALLY FRENCH' CORRUGATED-IRON 2CV PICK-UP WAS A PRODUCT OF CITROËN'S UK SLOUGH FACTORY; AN ATTEMPT TO ENTICE BRITISH FARMERS TO GO METRIC.

THE TIN SNAIL THAT WENT TO WAR

The Citroën 2CV has a rightful niche in the classic car 'Hall of Fame,' and, whilst viewed by many as a quirky outsider, there is an even quirkier British derivative with a military bearing that deserves a mention: the 2CV pick-up.

Background

Citroën's UK Slough factory tried in vain from 1953 to convert the British to the Gallic minimalist motoring of the 2CV. Thirteen years after giving up the struggle, the idea caught on, and from 1974 Deux Chevaux sold well here in the UK.

During the 1950s, Slough had built French 2CV saloons and vans, but also tooled-up for a unique British pick-up. This variant was intended for rural activity,

and was therefore offered to *Farmers Weekly* for testing. The magazine noted the novel front-wheel drive, and tried it over ploughed fields and stubble when laden with bales of wet hay, but encountered no wheelspin. The pick-up could carry a useful 5cwt (254kg). *Farmers Weekly's* overall impression seemed to be one of bemusement, when comparing to the pick-up's more conventional contemporaries. Slough must have been reasonably pleased, however, as it reproduced the article for wider circulation.

Military service

Without further encouragement, pick-up production would probably have petered out before the end of the frustrating '50s, if the fickle finger of fate had not intervened. It was realised that this unlikely utilitarian device could just about be lifted by a military helicopter;

in fact, this may be the first example of such an airlift option. WW2 assault gliders, such as the Horsa, that delivered hundreds of jeeps, had been phased out, and military planners were struggling to exploit the obvious rapid deployment talents of the helicopter, despite their limited payload in the 1950s. By early 1957, the concept of Naval Commando Carriers was established, with helicopters replacing fixed-wing aircraft.

The Westland Whirlwind was able to pluck the just-over-10cwt (508kg) 2CV off the deck of an aircraft carrier, and deposit it at any required hot-spot. This was obviously a top level matter, as Duncan Sandys, the then Minister of Defence, attended a demonstration of the 2CV pick-up at Lee-on-Solent, Hampshire, in 1957.

The Light Fleet Carriers *HMS Bulwark* and *HMS Albion*, completed in the early 1950s, were converted to helicopter carriers in 1960 and 1962 respectively. Each carried a large contingent of Royal Marines, plus 16 helicopters. Slough built 35 of the 2CV pick-ups in 1960, and a further 30 in 1961, which ties in with these ships being fitted out for their new role. It seems rum now to picture an aircraft carrier with immaculate military rows of olive-green 2CVs on the flight deck, but that's exactly what happened.

The British Citroën 2CV pick-up was used by Royal Marine Commandos in places such as Aden, Malaya, and Borneo, and was also in use at a Middle East Royal Navy Base in 1963.

Period photographs show two pick-ups in rough country, carrying large radio transmitter/receivers. This would be an ideal way of exploiting the Citroën's amazing ability to absorb surface irregularities. No doubt, 1950s radio sets required all the cushioning they could get.

Novel features

Notwithstanding its unconventional appearance, it's worth remembering some of the 2CV's novel engineering features, which included a platform chassis with interconnected suspension employing mid-mounted spring units, inboard front brakes, two-cylinder air-cooled engine with no cylinder-head gaskets, and no distributor. It also possessed a starting-handle.

Most of the construction is close to a 'knock-down' approach, with bolt-on wings, lift-off doors, bonnet and boot lid (or tail-gate). Although the pick-up had proved air-portable, any further weight reduction obviously increased the helicopter's payload. Even the lightweight 2CV could be further lightened, and the military pick-ups were often used without doors and windscreens, and anything else that could be removed. Additional holes were cut each side of the small rear window, which would help with panic reversing in 'bandit country.' A lack of doors would also aid rapid ingress and egress.

This enthusiastic weight-reduction strategy must also have helped occupants remain cool in the tropics. In some cases, the lower rear bulkhead of the cabin was cut away, which, coupled with removal of the passenger seat, enabled a longer load to be carried. Some pick-ups were fitted with high level exhaust outlets running, truck-like, up the side of the cab. Bearing in mind the roll angles possible with the softly-sprung Citroën, it's not surprising that grab handles appeared on top of the cab!

As far as colours go, most of the vehicles used by the Royal Marines seem to have been painted dark,green: although the Royal Navy used dark blue paint, of course.

According to the chassis numbers in Malcolm Bobbitt's excellent *The British*

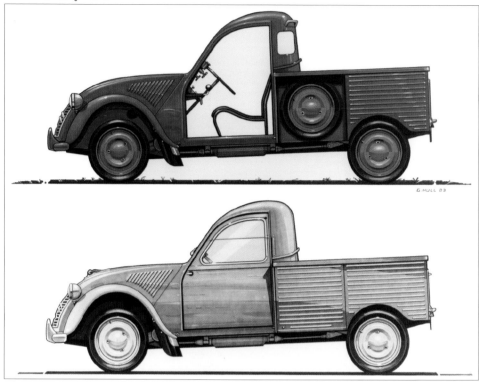

THE 2CV PICK-UP (LOWER) WAS TOO UNCONVENTIONAL FOR UK FARMERS, BUT IT COINCIDED WITH THE NEED TO MOTORISE HELICOPTER-BORNE MARINES; HENCE THE MILITARY VARIANT (TOP).

Citroën, a total of 131 2CV pick-ups were built between 1953 and 1961. Nearly as rare as hen's teeth, I saw one in the early '60s being thrashed flat-out past Blackbushe aerodrome. Another, frequently seen in 1968, was owned by an art student in Swinging London, and used to carry large pieces of sculpture. Flaunting mismatched doors and no tailgate, it had probably been demobbed.

Mysterious demise

Having been used operationally by the military for several years, there is little account of the circumstances of the pick-up's demise. The chassis of the 2CV would be capable of soaking up serious punishment, but I'm not so sure about the body. Some mention is made of badly damaged, carrier-based examples being dispatched to Davy Jones' locker.

No doubt four-wheel drive and more power would have been desirable. These Citroëns would have had only 425cc with which to face the opposition, because it was some years and another era before the unburstable flat-twin engine could boast 602cc.

One source in The Wessex Intensive Flying Unit at RNAS Culdrose recalls three Citroëns being used as general transport during 1964-65; remembered for heroic roll-angles. These particular pick-ups were replaced by Steyr-Puch Haflingers, the 4x4 mechanical mountain goats which could apparently tow helicopters.

The Ministry of Defence requested an air-portable Land Rover with a maximum weight of 2500lb (1134kg),

GH.14

EARLY HELICOPTERS STRUGGLED TO LIFT ANYTHING OTHER THAN THEMSELVES, BUT THE 10cwt (508kg) 2CV PICK-UP WAS LIGHTER THAN THE OBVIOUS FIRST CHOICE LAND ROVER.

To Boldly Go

but, despite drastic efforts, Land Rover could not get the vehicle's weight below 2650lb (1202kg). However, by the time the lightweight SWB Land Rovers were delivered in 1968, helicopters had sufficient engine power to lift them.

Reflection

There are other contenders for the rarest, most unusual vehicle variant – not least of which is the twin-engine 2CV – although the Deux Chevaux pick-up takes a bit of beating. The next time you see a Citroën 2CV, reflect for a moment on a time when a unique British version of a car that had come to epitomise quirky French design was slung under helicopters, and went into action for Queen and country.

To Anglicise the 2CV, Slough-built cars were fitted with chromed hub caps: which, traversing an uneven railway level crossing, our car's agitated wheels shed most of. An embarrassed passenger (you've guessed who) had to go and retrieve the caps, apologising to the innocent bystanders.

The 2CV Sahara 4x4 had an additional engine and transmission in the boot. The still-lightweight car dealt well with desert sands for oil exploration duties.

The AZP pick-up with the 425cc engine was produced from 1955-1961. The AP pick-up had been built from 1953-1955 with just 375cc of power.

FIAT 500
1957-1975

HULL 02

DESPITE ITS ECONOMY-CAR PERSONA, THE 1957 FIAT 500 ATTRACTED THE ATTENTION OF TUNERS; PARTICULARLY ABARTH'S 595cc AND 695cc VERSIONS.

THE MOUSE THAT COULD EVENTUALLY BE COAXED INTO ROARING

Those who believe that they have got the appeal of cars all figured out should consider the 1957-1975 Fiat 500, which is especially relevant in light of subsequent solutions to providing motoring for the masses.

Against the backdrop of the likes of Ferrari and Porsche, there are clubs for absolutely anything and everything on wheels – even the most unlikely of them – whose owners wear their anoraks with pride, drink milk straight from the bottle, and make trainspotters look like members of the Really Dangerous Sports Club. It is impossible, however, to dismiss Fiat 500 devotees as such. Michael Schumacher, to name one, was

not ashamed to be seen behind the wheel of a 500; Gordon Murray, chief engineer of the legendary McLaren F1, hasn't disguised his feelings for this ingenue's charms, and F1 designer Peter Stevens made a kind of open version of the Fiat. (Remember, these are all people who regard 450bhp as a reasonable starting point.) The tiny Cinquecento is a car that might rattle when passed by a milk float with low batteries.

Background
The first Fiat 500 was the Topolino of 1936-1955: a small, two-door vehicle employing a 569cc, water-cooled front engine. This was followed by the Fiat 600 of 1955-1969, with its water-cooled, rear-mounted, 633cc (eventually 843cc) engine.

Both cars were successful, but the Fiat 500 of 1957 outshone them both in the long run. For what might be regarded as

To Boldly Go

a city car became more the Italian Mini, and used throughout that country.

From a groundbreaking engineering design aspect it cannot be compared to 'people's cars' such as the VW Beetle, Citroën 2CV or, of course, Issigonis' Mini, but, as is the nature of such things, this is what the bambino Fiat became in Italy, and no less iconic.

Mechanicals

The Turin car is 2.7cwt (137kg) lighter than a 1959 Mini, due to the Fiat's smaller, vertical, parallel-twin, air-cooled engine. Originally of 13bhp (479cc), and

then 17bhp (499cc), it finally grew to a 23bhp, 594cc unit. The suspension is quite simple, with a transverse leaf spring at the front and coil springs at the rear. It has drum brakes all round, and worm and sector steering.

An interesting variant was the estate, which, to create a flat rear loading bay, had the engine on its side under the floor, where – apparently – it continued to function.

Body

The Fiat 500 in question is a diminutive, rear-engine, two-door, four-seater. It is

SIMILAR TO MODIFIED MINIS, THE FIAT CINQUECENTO WAS TAKEN TO EXTREMES, WITH CARBURETTORS AND OIL COOLERS SPILLING OUT OF THE BOOT. THE RED SCORPION WAS A BRILLIANT TRADEMARK.

3.5in (89mm) shorter than the 1959 Mini, and of similar height, although appears taller. Using a conventional steel monocoque, early versions had rear-hinged 'suicide' front doors, and an opening, fabric roof was standard. There is a small boot at the front, which accommodates the fuel tank, spare wheel, and very thin handbook.

In the field

Aesthetically, the 500 is perhaps the most perfectly resolved small car shape ever; a great example of a continuous surface form. From whichever direction you look, the shapes flow seamlessly around the vehicle. Essentially a layered wedding-cake design building from the base up, three diminishing tiers culminate in the roof. So considered is the solution, that the original wooden tooling master-stack has been exhibited at the Science Museum. On this body, you could turn loose the world's finest clay modellers, and the best surfacing computers, and struggle to find a reason to change a millimetre.

Italdesign's Giorgetto Giugiaro has paid homage to the 500's shape with a delightful painting of the rear quarter

side panels. His spiritual successor to the Fiat, the Daewoo Matiz, used the same wedding-cake 'stack' to good effect.

An avid fan of the Fiat 500, even before regular business trips to Italy, it seems to the author to encapsulate, in miniature, the essence of Italian design. There is a classless fusion of art and engineering, which expresses an undeniable joie de vivre. A dusty example outside an ochre-painted, red-pantiled farmhouse in Turin's hinterland shows its roots, yet a gleaming example in London's Kensington Church Street is equally at home.

The light steering and minimum dimensions make light work of tight manoeuvring. The slight seats are surprisingly comfortable, and four close friends wearing T-shirts can be accommodated. One is aware of sharing a metal box with a basic 'motorbike' engine which, when extended (ie always), sounds uncouth, frankly. Even the glass-half-full brochure dares claim only 59mph for the 499cc unit.

The irresistible urge

Considering its guileless simplicity, this vehicle, from its arrival in the late 1950s, has been obsessively interfered with. Every trick in the many-paged Italian tuning book has been used to wring extra power from the concrete mixer-sounding motor: carburettors bolted on that are so big you cannot shut the boot lid, and exhaust pipes up which you can almost see the valve-gear. Cars converted by the likes of Abarth and Giannini are now collector's items. The genuine Abarth 595SS and 695SS are virtually unobtainable, their owners creeping down to heated garages in the small hours to gloat over them. Just thinking about a large capacity, alloy-finned sump hanging down under the rear bodywork, and bearing the word 'Abarth' in big, red

letters, makes fans feel good. The sting-in-the-tail scorpion badge warns others that this little device threatens to bite … your ankles.

Carlo Abarth was born in Austria, and, ironically, Italian tuning companies were upstaged in the hot Fiat 500 stakes by another Austrian source, Steyr-Puch, whose cars were a unique and potent cocktail of Fiat 500 bodyshell and Austrian mechanics.

The modified Fiat 500 cult has retained its disciples over the years. An otherwise rational Royal College of Art design student, exposed to an Abarth 595, got the bug really badly. He was rumoured to have abandoned his flat, and locked himself in a Shepherd's Bush railway arch garage with this car for over a year. It emerged, hugely modified, lowered to the ground, with wide alloy wheels, bulging wheelarches and 800cc Gozzoli barrels inserted.

Enthusiasts continue to shoehorn various power units into the gamine waif's engine compartment, including a Subaru flat-four: so much torque, so little weight, there was probably no need for a gearbox. One guy began a perfectly reasonable restoration, and ended up dipping the entire bodyshell in a giant galvanising tank; then, surrendering entirely to some primitive urge, modified the engine so effectively it was constantly shearing the driveshaft flange bolts.

Food for thought

Considering the awesome sums of money that have gone into creating modern motor cars, it's surprising that more use is not made of behavioural psychologists. The diminutive Fiat and its followers would make an interesting case study, in this instance. The model is mechanically obsolete, has no virility rating, and, even when force-fed on steroids, can barely match the humblest entry models of today.

What it does have, of course, and which melts the hearts of some of the toughest car nuts, is that elusive automotive phenomenon – charisma. It's thought-provoking to consider that several later Fiat 126s could be had for the price of a single original 500. The 126 was the all-round superior replacement to the 500, but possessed zero visual panache. Many sound examples suffered the ignominy of having their 650cc engine and gearbox torn out, and used to rejuvenate much older Fiat 500s. This brand manager's nightmare scenario is exactly echoed by the Citroën Dyane. Perhaps the best light car ever, the Dyane could not upstage the iconic 2CV it was based on, and intended to replace.

The visual appeal of the original Fiat 500 is so strong that, 32 years after its demise, the shape was resurrected. The 2007 re-release, or cover version, proved a time warp hit all over again. Although the born-again BMW Mini and VW Beetle also aped their originals, the Fiat looks the most faithful, albeit pumped-up and front-engined front-wheel drive. Slightly odd that the wedding cake side-section

was changed to an overhang, but it's the same DNA. The copy is an automotive example of 'the singer not the song,' or, as the Americans would say, if something looks good, it *is* good.

Conclusion

It is a peculiar truth that travel is as much about the means as the geography. Anyone who enjoys driving can savour the energy management challenge of coaxing maximum return from minimum assets, and, whether standard or modified, the Fiat 500 is a founder member of this club.

The shape of the 1957-75 Fiat 500 is irresistibly cute. For some reason the clockwork toy persona of its rudimentary engine seems to bring out one's protective instincts; when pressed hard the car seems to be asking "Why are you doing this to me?" Paradoxically, there is also an element of "Well, if you insist, you could always tune me a bit!"

A side effect of describing such cars is the possibility of an attack of semi-crazed enthusiasm. Where is that list again? Abarth-lowered springs, Campagnolo-style alloy wheels, Dell'Orto carburettor, disc brake conversion …

Although the standard 499cc was all done at 59mph, in April 1967 *Motor* magazine did briefly record 64.3mph. This could, of course, have been just 'wild talk' around the coffee machine …

Car magazine, in a novel group test in November 1965, achieved 59mph in the Fiat and 62.4mph in a 598cc Reliant Regal three-wheeler.

MESSERSCHMITT
KR200
1955-1964

TARGETING SOLID GERMAN CITIZENS TOO POSH FOR A SCOOTER BUT NOT WEALTHY ENOUGH FOR A CAR, THE MESSERSCHMITT BUBBLECAR EVENTUALLY ACHIEVED ICONIC STATUS.

KABINENROLLER

This Messerschmitt was, and remains, the most evocative example of the bubble car genre; a tiny, instantly recognisable, three-wheeled tandem-two-seater, bearing one of aviation's most potent brand names.

Background

Fritz Fend, a young Luftwaffe technical officer, had specialised in undercarriage design: a particularly crucial role when one considers the last-minute need to convert the Messerschmitt 262 jet fighter from tail-wheel to nose-wheel. 1945 found Fend on the run from the Allied press gangs: just as the Nazis had pillaged European art treasures, the Allies now pillaged German aeronautical treasures – jet designs and their designers. One can argue that the Russian MiG 15 and American F-86 Sabre

aircraft that battled over Korean skies during 1950-53, each owed something to Focke-Wulf and Messerschmitt concepts. Von Braun, who developed the V2 rocket at Peenemünde, was scooped up by the Americans, and played a key role in man landing on the moon. Fend chose to keep his head down, working on a farm.

From the ashes

At the end of the Second World War, survivors of a ruined Germany were picking around in the rubble. Amongst the human casualties were significant numbers of disabled servicemen.

By 1947 Fend had secured a small workshop, where he began to experiment with ultra-simple personal transport – a 'Flitzer' (meaning to dash along): a man-powered tricycle employing cranks and levers which could also be used by the disabled.

This became first semi-enclosed then fully enclosed and, in 1948, powered. Later Flitzers had a 98cc, 4.5hp Riedel two-stroke engine (a Me 262 starter motor), and wheelbarrow wheels replaced the earlier bicycle wheels – dire days, indeed.

Producing ten cars a week, Fend wanted to expand and further develop the concept. In 1952 he approached his old employers for financial help to develop a two-seat, streamlined, enclosed, three-wheeled scooter. Messerschmitt was banned from aircraft production, and its Regensburg factory was reduced to repairing railway wagons. Prof Willy Messerschmitt remembered Fend's aircraft work, and convinced the Board to help him.

Fend's resulting Kabinenroller KR175 appeared at the 1953 Geneva Show. As before, it had two wheels at the front and one at the rear; a 175cc engine, and a mixture of car and motorcycle controls. It featured fully-enclosed front wheels and a sideways hinged plastic dome incorporating a glass windscreen. The model was reasonably successful, selling around 9000 units over two years. It was exported to numerous countries, including America, but needed refining, both technically and aesthetically. Exactly who did what in the following two years is debatable; it's probable that Messerschmitt, sensing the potential, gave Fend quite a lot of design support, and in 1955 the very well resolved KR200 was launched.

Construction and equipment

Think aircraft, and Messerschmitt's philosophy of 'Weglassen' (paring a design to minimum weight while retaining strength) and you have the KR, the heart of which was a torsionally-rigid steel tube and pressings tub, in which the occupants sat. Integral with the front floor was a box crossmember, carrying the swinging-arm suspension units.

Engine and suspension were retained by a steel tube frame cantilevered off the rear bulkhead (pure aircraft technique), while the rear wheel was located by a cast alloy trailing arm, that also enclosed the drive chain in an oil bath. The hinged boot contained the fuel tank, spare wheel, and small stowage compartment.

The fixed nose pressing carried two headlamps, and the bolted-on front wings had wheel cut-outs, allowing maximum track and lock. Suspension was rubber-in-torsion all round with dampers.

Unlike the KR175, all controls were car-type, as steering was previously direct via new, ergonomically-shaped handlebars. Gear change was sequential, with a trigger for neutral selection. A dynastart (starter and generator) allowed the engine to run backwards for reverse.

The split rear seat allowed a suitcase (or a small, unnaturally well-behaved child) to be accommodated beside the passenger. If required, a luggage rack could be bolted onto the boot. There was a choice of roofs: a perspex 'bubble,' a folding canvas hood, a frameless windscreen for the KR201 with hood and removable side screens, or just a fly-screen and tonneau for the KR Sport. Very much forward control, the driver's seat could be pulled up and back on parallelogram links; the driver then lowered himself down and forward (most drivers simply jumped in).

The 191cc Sachs two-stroke developed 9.7bhp at 5000rpm – enough to propel a vehicle weighing just 506lb (230kg) at a smart pace. The KR's coefficient of drag was tested at Cd 0.4 in VW's wind tunnel: good for 1955. The small frontal area and flat underside were ideal; aerodynamic drag depends on the size of the hole being punched through the air and any associated turbulence: the little Messerschmitt scored well on both counts.

The packaging of the KR200, its structural integrity, build quality, and purchase and running costs immediately appealed, and it sold well.

The record breaker

In late August 1955, a streamline version of the new KR200 was wheeled out to challenge several records at Hockenheim racetrack. This was, essentially, the production vehicle, but with a single-seat cockpit, sculptured aero screen, head fairing, low drag front wings, and softened lower front edges. Regulations required ballast for passenger weight.

The 191cc engine had raised compression, polished ports, and modified carburettor, all producing 14bhp at 5500rpm. A smaller rear drive sprocket raised gearing slightly. Additional scoops and vents helped engine cooling, and a long expansion-box exhaust rudely stuck out the back.

Beating the previous 250cc and 350cc records, Fend, with five other drivers, averaged 64mph for 24 hours, at times pulling 77.7mph on the straights. A 72mph lap was possible, but reliability was paramount. These days, we are blasé about such speeds, but, in 1955, it was going some for a littl'un.

Painted white with blue graphics, this machine was perfect for promotional purposes. It emphasised Fend's confidence that he had found a unique niche, not an apology for a car, or a breadline cycle-car, and superior to a scooter.

What was the KR200 like on the road?

Half the appeal of unconventional vehicles is that the driving experience is always memorable. The Sachs engine was smooth, and, like all two-strokes, once you found the sweet spot in the relatively narrow power band, the KR accelerated through the gears surprisingly well. Like Lambretta and Vespa scooters, high revs and associated engine note gave a sporty and fun feel to progress. Top gear, like many low-powered continental vehicles, felt high (4.22), so it was more like a three-speed gearbox with overdrive.

Top speed figure is contentious: journals and brochures range from 53mph to 70mph; this owner and others say maybe 62mph on the flat. Gradients are a factor, and two-strokes seem to like a little moisture in the air. Best to avoid violent de-acceleration scenarios with cable brakes, though they were up to stopping this very light vehicle (early VW Beetles had cable brakes). The direct 'go-kart' steering required familiarisation to avoid over-control. Fuel economy was excellent, at

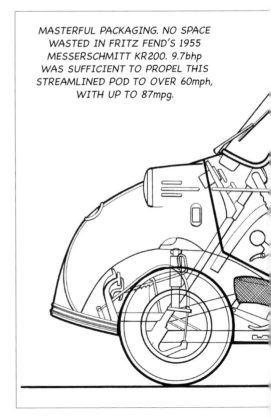

MASTERFUL PACKAGING. NO SPACE WASTED IN FRITZ FEND'S 1955 MESSERSCHMITT KR200. 9.7bhp WAS SUFFICIENT TO PROPEL THIS STREAMLINED POD TO OVER 60mph, WITH UP TO 87mpg.

65-87mpg, depending on the driver's testosterone levels.

The overriding feature was the tandem seating. The central driving position, as McLaren F1, enabled precise positioning of the 50in (1270mm) width. All-round visibility was exemplary. The 8in (203mm) wheels were not ideal for smoothing out bumps, but, like most light vehicles, it rode better laden.

This wind-cheating capsule cocooned you like no scooter, with or without a windscreen. The occupants sitting low and on the centre line gave great stability, and the KR cornered well with minimum roll. I guess the hinged canopy was fundamental to the experience, because, when opened, you knew it wasn't like a car or scooter or anything else. Anyone with the sailplane experience of sitting under a plastic canopy would acknowledge the aircraft DNA. It was impossible not to enjoy the KR200: it was just plain (plane) fun.

What happened, and why aren't we all driving them?

Having been involved with some of the world's most advanced aircraft, Fend was never going to settle for mediocrity. 1955 was a very good year for sales, and soon to be bolstered by the Suez oil crisis of 1956. But even as his little masterpiece was launched, the green shoots of Germany's postwar economic miracle were emerging. Soon, if you couldn't aspire to a VW Beetle, then other homegrown micro cars such as the 1954 Goggomobil, or 1957 NSU Prinz, etc, were waiting to step in, and could just about carry four people.

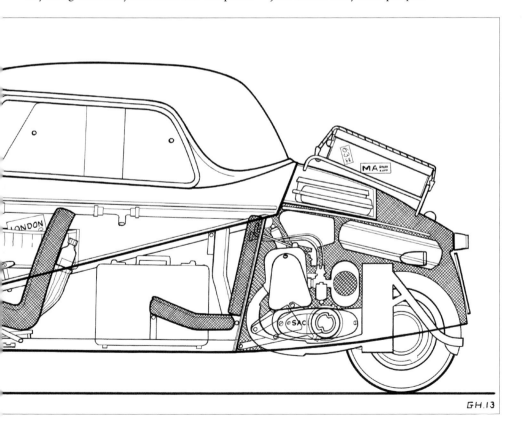

GH.13

To Boldly Go

Like all sagas there are twists and turns to explore before the final curtain: stuff happens, and the KR200 was a cork on life's ocean. Messerschmitt toyed with a Goggomobil-like prototype, the K106, but, despite Fend's attempts to raise funds, the idea stalled. Sales were good, but production costs were high, and a hurricane that damaged a big shipment to America didn't help. Politics added to the problems: the German government was willing to assist with Messerschmitt's return to aircraft production, but feared the car business would leech funds, so decreed it be sold off.

In 1957, Fend, in partnership with one of his suppliers, formed Fahrzeug und Maschinenbau Regensburg (FMR). An FMR badge had to replace the eagle symbol on the nose, because Mercedes claimed it looked like its three-pointed star. In turn, Auto Union complained that the initials FMR, in three interlocked circles, looked like its own four interlocked circles, forcing the change to interlocked diamonds. Taking pity on its bullied former colleague, Messerschmitt allowed Fend to retain its name on the cabin.

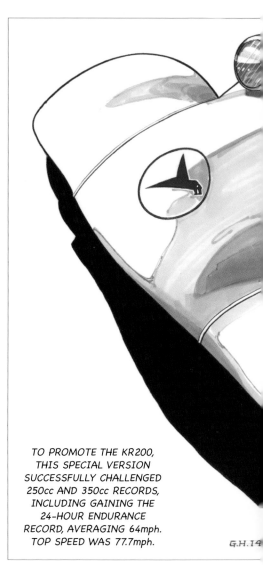

TO PROMOTE THE KR200, THIS SPECIAL VERSION SUCCESSFULLY CHALLENGED 250cc AND 350cc RECORDS, INCLUDING GAINING THE 24-HOUR ENDURANCE RECORD, AVERAGING 64mph. TOP SPEED WAS 77.7mph.

G.H.14

	1961	1963
KR200	£345	£349
Isetta	£360	£325
Heinkel/Trojan	£370	£370
Austin Mini	£497	£448
Goggomobil	£467	£399
NSU Prinz	£547	–
VW Beetle	£617	£625
Tg500	£666	–
BMW 700	–	£698
(UK prices include purchase tax)		

The new company lacked funds for developing a rival to the growing breed of mini cars, but, in 1958, a four-wheeled 'KR' was launched: the Tg500 (see next chapter). By now, however, price comparisons with other models were painting a bleak picture, as shown in the table on the left.

In the UK young couples were buying £360 Minivans in their droves (no purchase tax). Why would you prefer a tiny, two-stroke-powered,

tricycle to this? It was all over, bar the shouting. Researchers estimate that around 25,000 KR200s were produced, and the UK was the largest export market at about 5000 units, with 1958/59 the prime years. By the end of 1963, when Fend left to concentrate on consultancy work, the sales decline was terminal.

Rebirth – star of stage and screen
The rollcall of celebrities associated

with the KR200 is a long one; Elvis Presley, Red Arrows pilots, Dick Emery (comedian), Jon Pertwee (*Doctor Who*), Terry Gilliam in his film *Brazil*, are but a few. The KR appeared in many television programmes, and even on billboard adverts, being driven by a German with a spiked helmet. It has also been displayed in numerous public places, including the Design Museum and the Science Museum in London. Because the car is instantly recognised, its visual appeal doesn't appear to fade: it has achieved that rare plateau of iconic design. Even replicas were made in the 1990s. KR200 auction prices continue to defy logic.

Conclusion

Fend's 1955-1964 'Flitzer' worked on several levels:

- It was a unique, superbly engineered and packaged cabin scooter. It was a lot better than a scooter, and had some advantages over a car – eg, purchase price, running costs and parking.
- It balanced form and function perfectly. Given a similar design brief, it's hard to imagine much in the way of improvement. Aesthetically, it's a design in the round, and no camera angle catches out its styling. It's a classic case of 'if it looks right, it probably *is* right.'
- It was fun to drive, and always more than just transport, as witnessed by numerous sporting events in Germany. In the UK, Ken Piper, successfully campaigned KRs in competition events for Testwood Motors; others enjoyed equal success. If enthusiasts take to a vehicle, usually, some form of motorsport beckons.

The KR200 was a rational purchase during the austerity years of the 1950s, but its sought-after classic status is infinite. Never bettered, never equalled, Fritz Fend lived to witness the continuing affection for his small but perfectly formed invention, and met many of his fans at special events. *Autocar's* Jeff Daniels, writing in 1977, declared it "one of the most remarkable minimum car designs put into production."

One cannot discuss the story of Fend's babies without mentioning certain UK individuals – people like Conrad Moore, John Perkins and Phil Boothroyd. All were devotees of both the three- and four-wheeler. Like true marque enthusiasts, they regarded themselves as temporary custodians of these vehicles, which, following their owner's passing, transferred to the care of other like-minded individuals. It's one thing to jump on a bandwagon, but these three cherished Fend's work from day one. It's not necessary to analyse why certain vehicles get under your skin. They just do.

When hard-pressed for long periods, two-strokes have been known to seize. The fuel and oil mix is critical, which is why motorcycle racers tended to keep two fingers on the clutch lever. The KR200 handbook acknowledged this, and instructed 'If the engine seizes, allow it to cool down for the time it takes to smoke a cigarette,' conjuring up the image, perhaps, of a gloved hand holding a cigarette, eyes half-closed in bliss.

The Kabinenroller's link to aircraft design tends to be played down, but the canopy is hinged on the same side as the Me109 and Me262 fighters. Single-seat cockpits are mostly entered from the left wing: handy for the UK, but the Continent? Horses are generally mounted from the left, so are bicycles and motorbikes; makes you think, doesn't it ...

Brockbank, the inspired cartoonist, found this cabin scooter irresistible, featuring it several times in his images. One showed a KR on the deck of a canal boat, Rhine barge-style; another, a frustrated courting couple having to drive past Lover's Lane ...

A KR175 living in North Harrow had 'Die Fledermaus' neatly written alongside its cockpit; another KR was seen driven down Harrow High Street, the rear occupant blowing a bugle out of the rear window – a perfectly reasonable event in the 1960s.

10
FMR Tg500 (MESSERSCHMITT TIGER)
1958-1961

THE REAR END WAS UNIQUE TO THE TG500: A 500cc, TWO-STROKE TWIN, CAPABLE OF OVER 80mph. INHERENTLY STABLE, ITS ABILITY TO TACKLE TIGHT BENDS AND SLALOMS OFTEN SHOCKED ONLOOKERS.

AND NOW FOR SOMETHING COMPLETELY DIFFERENT

December 19th 1958: *Autocar* magazine road-tested a Tg500, registration UHO 505, and wasn't hugely impressed. In March 1959, UHO 505 appeared on the cover of *Motor Sport* after winning a prestigious UK rally, and in February 2013, a Tg500 was sold at auction in America for $322,000 (including buyer's premium and sales tax). Did *Autocar* get it wrong? We have to go back to the 1950s to understand this enigmatic and legendary bubblecar.

Background

The Messerschmitt KR200 cabin scooter three-wheeler was a clever way of using a small engine to propel two people, protected from the elements, with a degree of flair and fun. Born out of economic necessity, its initial success was eclipsed by the rapidly rising aspirations of a Germany recovering from the Second World War. Fritz Fend, the vehicle's designer, when forced to leave the umbrella of Messerschmitt proper, wanted to profit from the growing desire to own saloon cars. Despite his efforts to diversify and develop new designs, he couldn't raise the funds, however. His KR200, although achieving good early sales, had never been very profitable, and its life cycle was limited. Given the three-wheeler's surprisingly sporty character, a 'variant' majoring on this aspect wasn't such a leap of the imagination; hence the additional wheel, and bigger engine, of the Tg500.

How the Tg500 differs from the KR200

Despite their similar DNA, the Tg and KR wouldn't have mated in the wild.

To Boldly Go

KR pressings were used where possible, but often with significant modifications, and the superstructure was a carryover. The running gear, engine and transmission had virtually nothing in common.

The KR's scooter wheels were replaced by 10in (254mm) items, pre-empting the Mini. The Tg's front track is 1in (25.4mm) wider than the KR's; the rear track 2in (50.8mm) narrower than the KR's front. Front suspension and steering were similar, but beefed-up and hydraulic brakes replaced the KR's cables. Nothing is shared behind the rear bulkhead, which has a cantilevered tubular frame carrying the independent suspension and power unit. The latter was designed by Fichtel & Sachs, and built by FMR – a 490cc twin two-stroke engine producing 20bhp at 5000rpm, with a non-synchromesh four-speed and reverse gearbox. The engine side of the bulkhead carried a large fuel tank requiring a fuel pump, with the battery mounted on top of the tank. Between the engine and tank is a dynastart unit with twin cooling fans.

Rear suspension employed an asymmetric swing-arm wishbone invented by Fend, incorporating self-compensating toe-in geometry, reminiscent of that on the Porsche 928. Front and rear suspension was adjustable, and the vehicle could be raised or lowered with associated positive or negative camber. A bucket seat for the driver helped deal with cornering forces.

The spare wheel lived on the back of the modified KR boot, on top of which a luggage rack could be bolted. Headlamps, larger than the KR's, featured an attractive polished bezel. The Tg tipped the scales at 770lb (350kg).

That *Autocar* road test

Given that *Autocar* road tests are highly respected for their technical accuracy and unbiased analysis, its 1958 report

FINANCIALLY UNABLE TO MOVE ON FROM BUBBLECARS TO SALOONS, FRITZ FEND WORKED AT REGENSBURG TO UPGRADE THE KR200 TO A MORE POWERFUL FOUR-WHEELER – THE FMR Tg500. (ILLUSTRATIONS BY IAN KENNEDY)

on Fritz Fend's latest creation must have dismayed FMR, agents, and enthusiasts alike. *Autocar*'s final conclusion was damning by faint praise and dismissal:

"It would seem that the Tg500 must have limited appeal in this country, at a price swollen by import duty and purchase tax to over £650. Performance, particularly acceleration, is good for a 500cc car, but few sports car enthusiasts would approve of the steering or gear change. Although tandem seating is acceptable in a low cost economy runabout, a less freakish and more spacious layout is required for the serious motoring that is expected from a four-wheeler."

Ouch! Apart from anything else, *Autocar*'s best top speed was 68mph, whereas its English brochure optimistically claimed 90mph, and the German version read 130km/h (81mph).

For those who came to understand the Tg, there was one telling sentence buried in the text: "A notable feature of the car is the way it can be almost thrown round bends – the Tg500 can be cornered very fast indeed with complete absence of roll." The reader may reflect that exaggeration and hyperbole were not *Autocar*'s style.

In the event

Emphasising its sporty nature, Fend personally launched the Tg in the UK on Monday 29th September 1958 at Brands Hatch, with such sports press illuminati as John Bolster in attendance. The previous day, Fend had taken the device to Narborough, Leicestershire, for the benefit of the Messerschmitt Owners' club (MOC).

Testwood Motors at Southampton was the main UK importer. Given the price it was expected to sell this vehicle for, and the wet blanket *Autocar* had thrown

over the Tg500, the dealership must have wondered what to do, but took the bold step of campaigning demonstrators from various forms of motorsport – after all, the brochure strapline was 'The Phenomenal Sports car.' Testwood approached one Ken Piper, at the time racing 500cc grass track sidecar outfits, knowing direct steering would hold no fear for him. Ken kindly sent me a list of some of his 1959 results:

Exeter Trial	First class award and special award – 'Absolute best performance of all competitors'
Cat's Eyes Rally	Best performance award, outright winner, no marks lost
Snowstorm Rally	Outright winner
Lands End Trial	First class award and special award
Express and Star Rally	First prize
Bournemouth Rally	Class winner
London Rally	Harridine Trophy
Derbyshire Trial	Class winner
Scottish Rally	2nd in class, 7th overall
Taunton Motor Club Rally	First class award
Great Yarmouth National Rally	First class award

Ken Piper was, of course, competing in the up to 1000cc and 1300cc classes. If those using Austin Healey Sprites and VW Beetles, etc, were annoyed at being beaten by this previously ridiculed bubblecar, imagine the reactions of some of the more powerful opposition. Many complained that the Tg500 wasn't really a proper car at all!

Ken has pages of Tg's German sporting involvement, including circuit racing and hillclimbs, for which Fritz Fend's name often appeared. Significantly, in March 1961, there was a report of Ken retiring with technical problems in an Oxford University MC night rally; the winner being the new 850cc Mini with a John Sprinzel conversion. Second was a Triumph TR3A; third a Morgan Plus 4 – another giant killer had turned up … Ken continued to compete in as many events as possible, most effective where the Tiger's handling gave advantage, including all the principal hillclimb and auto test venues.

Following Ken Piper's extraordinary competition successes in 1959 and

beyond, Testwood's demonstrators found their way into the hands of UK privateers, who enthusiastically competed with them, mainly in trials.

Fully covering the Tg's sporting endeavours is beyond the scope of this chapter, unfortunately, but, as ever, the owners were at least as interesting as their steed. George Duller, ex-jockey and one of the original 'Bentley Boys,'

was an owner. Tommy Wood, a 1950s motorcycle racer, including success on the Isle of Man TT course, enjoyed attacking impossible Trials hills, day or night. Clifford Morrell, a Trials veteran, missed his first Tg so much after selling it that he bought another one. Clifford won a time prize in a London to Edinburgh event, and generally took the fight to the opposition with his ex-Testwood Tigers. His description of destroying a clutch on a violent hill start speaks volumes about his chosen branch of motorsport. Current UK owners have raced Tgs on the Nürburgring club circuit, and in other events. These pocket rockets have competed in handicap events at Silverstone, Goodwood and Mallory Park.

The RAC finally caught up with this irritating little aberration in the 1970s, banning it from production car events by enforcing a minimum cockpit width rule – one way of beating it round the bollards.

The car's record on the continent is too long to do justice to. One Hans Friesnig raced against Niki Lauda's Mini, and 50 years on still competes in the same Tg in Austrian hillclimbs, and a Tg won a European slalom championship. Fritz Fend was a successful competitor, including in grass track events and hillclimbs, etc.

The market place

Commercially, the car was virtually a non-starter, for which some blame the price; others a lack of supply. It cost about the same as, say, the Austin-Healey Sprite or VW Beetle, but the 1959 Mini was £150 less. Eighteen Tgs are quoted as being sold in the UK, nine of which were used in competition. Around 320 units is the

OF THE 18 UK-IMPORTED Tg500S, NINE WERE USED IN COMPETITION, WINNING MANY PRESTIGIOUS AWARDS AND PROVOKING CONTROVERSY. IT WAS EVENTUALLY BANNED.

lowest estimate of factory production by its end in 1961, and in 1966 13 examples were on the UK's MOC register.

KR enthusiasts rarely upgraded to the expensive Tg: four-wheeler road tax was £12.50, three-wheeler just £5. In addition, when the Tg was launched much cheaper used KRs were available, and could be driven by those holding a motorcycle licence.

The 1960s decline of bubblecars was rapid, and, although KRs survived until 1964, they had been slow out of the showroom. Remaining Messerschmitts owe their survival to dedicated clubs. Even if few KR owners would ever own a legendary Tiger, tales of their daring deeds were regularly told round the camp fire … well, club pub!

The ownership experience

As a teenager in the 1960s, I was practically given a 1958 KR200 convertible. Amongst my brochures was that of the fabled Tg500, a 100mph bubble car built for the Bavarian police. A college friend had been overtaken by one with four exhaust pipes on the M1! I'd never even seen this mystical beast: did it exist?

Tracking scant Tiger spoor led me to an architect in the MOC who had two, and he reluctantlt told me of a motorcycle dealer who had three! The North London Maida Vale backstreet establishment was memorable. Between a Porsche 356 and a kneeler sidecar outfit was a silver Tg with a blown up engine; outside was an immaculate British Racing Green example, and behind that the metallic-blue UHO 505, a Tiger desperately needing the RSPCA. Campaigned for eight years, it had a front trials tow-bar and, unnervingly, the paint on the mudguards was blistered by tyre contact. Due to its apparently exhausted state it was affordable. Shortly after my visit the establishment burnt down, but a green and a silver bubblecar somehow survived.

Despite 61,000 hard miles, UHO 505 was fine, except the gear change was punch-drunk. My father, a metalwork teacher, re-bushed the somewhat tortuous linkage, probably making it better than new in the process.

What was the Tiger like to drive?

The *Autocar* road test was clinically accurate; what it didn't spell out was that if you drove this car as if your trousers were on fire, its performance was extraordinary. Whether Fritz Fend planned it, or this was the inevitable outcome, a big-engined go-kart was what it was on the road. It may have looked like the three-wheeler plus an extra wheel, but it felt altogether more planted and serious.

Engine – A typical big two-stroke twin, the background whistle of its cooling fans making it sound as if it meant business.

Gearbox – Non-synchromesh gearbox wasn't ideal for a free-revving two-stroke, but open throttle down changes were a delight. Up changes weren't as slow as *Autocar* suggested, because competition cars had lightened flywheels, helping revs to fall. Third gear (4.75) was a compromise, and, as top was high (3.37), lack of torque forced a lot of use of third: narrow power bands need five- or six-speed boxes.

Brakes – The drum brakes were good – even fierce.

Steering/handling – Rear-engined cars often have little enthusiasm for travelling in a straight line, and direct steering exploited the car's inherent willingness to change direction quickly. Some 120 early cars had a dampermstrut fitted to the steering column to reduce 'sneeze factor' at speed, but most were removed. Tigers could adopt lurid, out-of-line controllable attitudes, because you never had to play 'catch-up' twirling a steering wheel. The vehicle always remained stable, despite the driver's most ruthless demands.

Performance

Competition Tigers strove for more power leading to non-standard pistons, lightened flywheels, modified carburation, padded crankcases (raising compression), polished ports, modified timing, and, in one case, removal of alternate fan blades. Close-ratio gears were available for hillclimbs. Two-strokes respond to tunable expansion-box exhaust systems, and a four tailpipe setup was available.

A legend's top-speed virility is always contentious, *Autocar*'s 68mph for UHO 505 seems unrepresentative.

Speaking as a passenger in one of the last Tgs, 80mph may be possible, this same vehicle in recent years employing the factory's front aerodynamic aid, and a blueprinted engine was timed by GPS as holding 85mph. Apparently rational owners feel comfortable cruising at 70mph, with forays into the 80s. It's nice to know they can do it, but the Tg's forte was always mid-range ability.

A lot depends on the engine's state of tune and weather conditions. For this soul, direct steering and gusting side winds focused attention on self-preservation, rather than top-speed heroics.

Aerodynamics

VW's wind tunnel measured the Tg's coefficient of drag as Cd 0.54, meaning it required about 35% more power at a

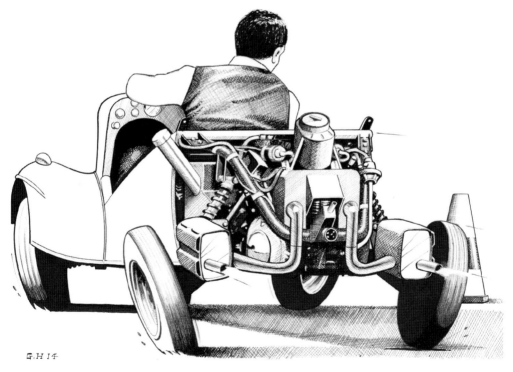

G.H 14

'MESSERSCHMITT TIGER' ACE, KEN PIPER, FURTHER PROVOKED CONTROVERSY BY SOMETIMES COMPETING WITH MUCH OF THE BODYWORK REMOVED. DESPITE THE REAR WHEELS ADOPTING EXTRAORDINARY ANGLES, THE VEHICLE REMAINED STABLE AND CONTROLLABLE.

given speed than did the three-wheeler. The small frontal area was excellent, but the rear wheel cowls created drag-inducing turbulence, which increased with the square of the speed. Today, the back end could be improved ... but we pass this way but once.

Summary and conclusion

The Tg500 remains an enigma: a bubblecar with the heart of a racer. FMR/Messerschmitt connoisseurs have referred to the Tiger as a prototype, ie not quite fully formed; the brochure, for instance, shows a different exhaust layout from production, and owners say no two Tigers look the same under the engine cover. In recent years a stiffer crankshaft and electronic ignition became available.

Fritz Fend's personal car, and those of others, had an unconventional, soft-nosed 'lip dam' which, it is claimed, gave significant fuel savings.

All of the foregoing are indications that the Tg might be considered a work-in-progress, just as the KR175 was before the KR200.

Conventional wisdom dictates that competition cars need very powerful engines, a wide track, wide tyres, and immensely powerful brakes. The Tg500 demonstrated that everything could be scaled down, gaining, in some circumstances, an advantage: add to the mix a talented driver and the results could be sensational.

Anyone using the Tg500 as a conventional car might be disappointed, but this fan remains in awe of what Ken Piper achieved in the late 1950s and early '60s. His trousers must have been well ablaze.

German giant Krupps claimed the rights to Tiger as a name, Tg was as close as FMR could get. It is fitting that this renegade always answered to the 'unofficial' name Messerschmitt Tiger.

Demonstrating the Tg500 to a MOC congregation in a quiet 1958 Sunday Narborough side road, Fritz Fend proved that the machine remained stable, despite trying to tear the tyres off the rims. So outraged was a local inhabitant by the spectacle that they called the Police!

"For demonstration purposes Ken takes it [UHO 505] down the road, with the speedo needle on 60mph, and throws it from lock to lock over and over again. In theory, it should turn over, but, in fact, it merely weaves in complete response to the steering." (*Motoring News*, April 2nd, 1959.)

"But out and out fastest man here was Ken Piper, who fairly snarled up with the Messerschmitt in 45.47. He produced a delightful 'pendulum' action with the tail, going left-right-left-right ... through the esses in perfect rhythm." Wiscombe Hillclimb, August 1960. (Commentator in local car club newsletter, *Exhaust Notes*.)

Ken Piper's competition success so impressed designer Fritz Fend that, whilst on a visit to Regensburg, Ken was 'given the keys' to the plant.

Indicating the green machine, Bob, the chap selling it, said "Ex-Clifford Morrell: he knew how to drive them," implying that some didn't. To demonstrate, a wild-eyed Bob climbed into UHO 505, with my father aboard (son observing), revs were gathered and the Tiger rocketed away to hurtle round a 90 degree left, still accelerating hard. It was like watching a speeded-up film: just as well my father's hair was already white ...

ISSIGONIS MINI

1959-2000

UNFORESEEN BY ITS CREATOR, SIR ALEC ISSIGONIS, THE MODIFIED MINI BECAME A PHENOMENON: EXPOSED ENGINE/GEARBOX, EXTREME SUSPENSION, AND WILD PAINT SCHEMES ALL PROJECTED PERSONAL EXPRESSION.

MAGICAL MYSTERY MINI

On hearing the word 'Mini,' many think of the BMW product, but it's worth reminding ourselves of the original Mini, and the influence of those who owned on today's motoring. However pivotal the Issigonis-designed Mini, the impact of those who drove it was at least as important; the main reason why getting from A to B is no longer the only consideration in car design.

Background

If the 1959 launch of the Mini was an automotive milestone, what happened next was a social phenomenon. The transformation occurred rapidly in the '60s. Musically, the Beatles were on fire, the Rolling Stones, Kinks, etc, also stocking the furnaces. Music was the immediate witness to the decade's seismic upheaval, but the era's effect on car design was deep and total. Individuals torched tradition and superimposed their own aspirations, morphing a utility vehicle into a lifestyle icon. The BMW Mini's aesthetics are a direct result of that public hijacking.

It started with the saloon car racing scene prising off the lid Pandora's box. Trips to Brands Hatch were brilliant, not only for the track action, but to see cars with *that* look on the road – lowered and widened suspension, straight through exhaust, dechroming, chunky steering wheels, and so on: the stuff of life. Steroids filtering down from the racing scene got into the automotive water table, adding a new twist to the automotive DNA spiral.

Minis, of course, were the darling of the 'In Crowd.' The car's cheeky giant-killer reputation in racing and rallying perfectly complemented the vortex of change blasting through this period. Not everyone could shake maracas on *Top of the Pops,* but a hot Mini showed willing. Apart from the racing influence, the luxury Mini interiors, 'Rolls-Royce' paint jobs, and Webasto roofs chosen by Peter Sellers, Ringo Starr, and the rest, kicked off today's feature-rich trend for even the most modest brands.

Fast Minis were not cheap, so anyone committed to serious modifications were either wealthy, reckless, or both. Cooper Ss were for the chosen few, and the smoothed, chopped-down Mini Sprints the absolute zenith of ultra cool. Others were lucky to get a basic Austin or Morris; even vans were candidates for white knuckle heroics.

Testimony

A Mini turned up on my patch of leafy suburban Harrow. This tired grey saloon was typical of what an enthusiast might get their hands on. It was stripped of badges, but hardly worth a second glance otherwise – just lowered, and track widened a bit, with Peco exhaust – small-time compared to swinging London's serious players.

Strangely enough, it was this Mini which would epitomise for me that swinging spirit, as the '60s became the '70s: a combination of *Street Fighting Man* meets *Urban Spaceman,* when individuals stepped into a parallel culture inspired by circumstance, flair and imagination. The marketplace began telling mass producers what it wanted.

Walking our Labrador along Pinner Road one night, a strange noise caught my attention. It wasn't Elton John practising his piano – he was about two miles up the road and still called Reg – this was a duet between the angry grunt of a tuned A-series engine, and the manic scream of a straight cut competition gearbox. As our inquisitive hound sniffed the air, a vision emerged from the night. Under the patchy sodium street lighting, a strange, almost frightening, object emerged ... a Mini so radically lowered, with the widest track imaginable, and extreme negative-cambered wheels, that it fused with its own shadow.

There was a brief impression of a crowded interior – two guys in the front, and maybe three girls in the back. The car was occasionally grounding, sending a shower of sparks flying in its wake, F1-style. It demonstrated that short, choppy ride of Alex Moulton's abused suspension when struggling to surmount the insurmountable.

I watched the car disappear around the long bend, knowing that this urban warrior had left an indelible image on my brain. Almost unbelievably, it was the old grey Mini, further modified and now sprayed in matt red primer – an emphatic 'No more, Mr Nice Guy' statement.

No doubt it was shrieking its way towards one of the local parties that the police attended at around 3am. Harrow had long been a haunt for pop groups such as Amen Corner, and The Who had regularly played at the Railway Hotel, Wealdstone, a couple of miles away. Charlie Watts had been at Harrow School of Art, and Screaming Lord Sutch was a local boy. The area had become known for creative social gatherings.

The next sighting of this extreme Mini machine occurred in the same road, when it was taking on petrol. The Mungo Jerry-haired, flared-trousered owner was understandably checking underneath the crouching, menacing creature. I weighed up the car whilst trying to act disinterested. Scorning alloys, it was on widened 10in (254mm) steels, and had no rear anti-roll bar or oil cooler – both usually found on mad-dog Minis.

These omissions seemed to increase the car's desperado appeal, as even the fundamental rules of cool were rejected: this really was a walk on the wild side of motoring.

A couple of weeks later, with a howl of exhaust and gears, a gold roof flashed past our garden hedge. It could only have been one vehicle, which must have been resprayed. I was surprised to see it park up the road. The sun sparkled crazily off of a dramatic metalflake two-tone paint job: the Mini in question was now gold down to its waist and red below. This visual trick emphasised the lowered look, and never better employed than here. The transformation from *Nowhere Man* to *Wild Thing* was complete.

The car lived just off the Pinner Road opposite the flats backing on to the Metropolitan Line, from where racing driver Piers Courage used to operate. On the tube every Monday morning, one could see the mangled nose-cones stacked against the embankment fence after a weekend's racing. For a short time in the '60s, before his unfortunate accident, Sir Frank Williams also hung out there.

Coming across the Mini one day, I was able to examine it at close quarters. The metalflake paint had huge aluminium particles, and the silver, steel wheels, on spacers had bands welded in, stretching across the widest tyres available. The extended arches were not the neat plastic extensions one might expect, but sheet metal (albeit blended in and colour-coded). The finned gearbox-cum-sump casing squatted precariously close to the road – sump guards were obviously for wimps. The retained rear bumper emphasised the car's width, and gave it a hint of conformity that might, maybe, satisfy a pursuing police car. The gold-painted engine and vital organs of starter motor, fanbelt, dynamo and distributor were rudely exposed – totally impractical, no doubt, in rain and dirt. Amongst sensible citizens this was an outlaw; the Hyde to Issigonis' Jekyll.

The interior was the complete antithesis of the pastel blue Mini we'd hired for a holiday. Leather-and-alloy steering wheel replaced shiny plastic.

MINIS WERE SOMETIMES EXPENSIVELY DE-SEAMED; ie, GUTTERS AND BODY JOINT FLANGES REMOVED. THIS EXAMPLE RELIED ON A DRAMATIC PAINT SCHEME TO GET STRAIGHT TO THE POINT.

POSSIBLY THE MOST MODIFIED CAR EVER IN ITS 1960S/1970S HEYDAY; THE MINI'S GIANT-KILLER RACING SUCCESS AND CHEEKY IRREVERENCE WERE A PERFECT ANTI-ESTABLISHMENT STATEMENT.

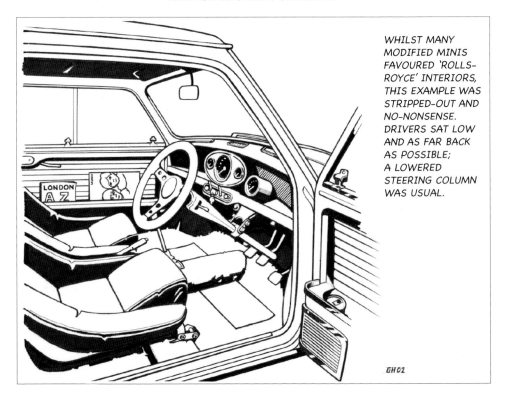

WHILST MANY MODIFIED MINIS FAVOURED 'ROLLS-ROYCE' INTERIORS, THIS EXAMPLE WAS STRIPPED-OUT AND NO-NONSENSE. DRIVERS SAT LOW AND AS FAR BACK AS POSSIBLE; A LOWERED STEERING COLUMN WAS USUAL.

It had a lowered steering column, well-worn but good bucket seats, and the usual extra instrumentation. The stubby Cooper gearlever was then still considered powerful magic, and completed the picture of a well-used but businesslike cockpit. Despite almost-psychedelic colours, this machine projected a ruthless efficiency. No frivolous stickers or trim, but, instead, a focused attitude – the raw side of 'Flower Power.'

I thought it totally inspired! It looked good, and got even better when in action, also suggesting a fun-loving lifestyle for its owner. This included the pop song ideal of boy meets girl; boy and girl run off together. The Kinks had told of 'Terry meets Julie at Waterloo Sunset,' Squeeze would one day dream of holidays complete behind the chalet. When the red-haired girl up the road walked, suitcase in hand, to that red-and-gold Mini it was, in my mind, to a Rolling Stones soundtrack. Perhaps the pair were simply going to the launderette, but, in my mind, their chariot would be screaming its way down to Brighton or Bognor.

The last time I saw the Mini was a classic moment. Jiggling slowly around a bend, it cruised past as I stood and followed its progress, admiring the perfect imagery. That great combination of outrageous, sun-splashed colour scheme and extreme mechanical commitment … I was a believer.

The owner, obviously aware of an audience, put on a little display, and the bi-coloured flat iron exploded into action, seeming to squat even lower and attacking the curve in style. Rumours about the diminutive demon's engine appeared well-founded. Exactly what had been done to it remains a mystery, but it was enough. In a crescendo of mechanical

SHOW AND GO. MODIFIED A–SERIES ENGINES RANGED FROM 850cc TO 1440cc. THE STRAIGHT-CUT GEARS AND STRAIGHT-THROUGH EXHAUST CREATED A MEMORABLE NOISE.

To Boldly Go

ferocity, with a hint of oil smoke and dust, the projectile exited stage left. It is one of my favourite recollections of magical Mini moments, along with the Works Cooper S cars imitating toboggans around an RAC forest stage.

Summary

The children of Issigonis' revolution reached for bigger engines and wilder wheels for their Minis. No surprise that the final production run was pumped-up Coopers – life imitating art. The '60s revolution caused a chain reaction that still has the marketplace demanding fun, magic, and excitement.

Today's cars owe their hearts to engineers, but their souls to the public. Issigonis' Mini is acknowledged for having worldwide influence, due to its transverse engine and front-wheel drive. But whenever you admire alloy wheels, or sit in a well-shaped seat gripping a chunky steering wheel and remote gearlever, remember those '60s enthusiasts who had their way.

Anyone asking why the Mini was so special would have no need to do so if they had witnessed that time of change. The Design Museum, or any car collection, should include a standard 1959 Mini, and a replica of its rogue, red-and-gold doppelgänger to explain all. As Ian McDonald said in his book *Revolution In The Head*, when summing up why the music of the Beatles era was so special: "Anyone with ears to hear, let them hear."

Minis were simply where it was at. A fellow design student gave me a lift into London in his mum's Mini. Being around the time of the Beatles' *Sgt Pepper's Lonely Hearts Club Band*, he was wearing the cardboard cut-out moustache from the LP's kit. Another Mini pulled alongside and, of course, the driver was wearing the same cut-out moustache.

A '60s *Autosport* magazine carried a 'For Sale' advert for a Mini van with, as was the custom, a long list of go-faster modifications, finally stating '120mph, according to Leicestershire police.'

Returning from Brands Hatch in a Hillman Imp, a much-modified, low-flying Mini overtook us, an oil cloud marking its passage. We re-passed it in a layby, its driver topping up the oil from a gallon (4.546 litre) can, while his girlfriend looked on. A little later, the mobile smoke screen went past again. None but the brave.

* * *

Let's leave the final word on the Mini to Alfred Lord Tennyson:

"The old order changeth, yielding place to new,
And God fulfils himself in many ways,
Lest one good custom should corrupt the world."

STEYR-PUCH HAFLINGER

1959-1975

THE LOW-GEARED 650cc ENGINE WAS HAPPIEST OFF-ROAD. IT WAS AVAILABLE IN SHORT AND LONG-WHEELBASE, WITH NUMEROUS BODY VARIANTS, INCLUDING AN ENCLOSED CAB, AND WAS USED FOR MANY MILITARY ROLES.

THE MOUNTAIN GOAT

Mention 4x4s, and various images and names are conjured up: mud-splattered genuine off-roaders, urban-jungle 'Chelsea tractors,' or, since the Audi Quattro, the rally special-stage weapon of choice.

A common theme running through today's 4x4s is a vehicle that projects power, and the capability to overcome all obstacles in its path; to boldly go where others dare not: a vehicle that can take on the most hostile environment and emerge the victor. It is not in tune with nature; nature is the enemy. It laughs in the face of rocks, fallen trees, mud, rivers, and impossible gradients: the chest-thumping Rambo of the automotive world. Brute

power turns huge tyres to propel unapologetically large superstructures through the worst thrown at it. Even on a suburban school run, it assumes the 'don't mess with me' shoulder-to-shoulder phalanx of bodyguards protecting a celebrity. All the more extraordinary, then, that one of the most effective 4x4s ever was a small, low-powered model that perched high on small wheels, had no body worth talking about, and appeared frightened of its own shadow.

Background

If we look at the evolution of all-wheel drive, the Willys Jeep is entitled to take a bow. This ubiquitous, go-anywhere, basic, lightweight, military vehicle was used and liked by all the armed forces. The Jeep's popularity continued long after World War Two, and, of course, influenced the 1948 Series One Land Rover, and those that followed. Land Rover picked up from where the Jeep left off, with a slightly more civilised body intended for farmers, and mixed terrain use. It was a good formula that remains a worldwide British success story over half a century later.

The Land Rover was no lightweight, using a massive chassis and two-litre engine, and was purposefully 'over-engineered' to such an extent that its weight frustrated attempts by early military helicopters to make it air-portable. 4x4 off-roaders have become synonymous with large, powerful machines capable of overcoming anything nature can muster, overriding each and every obstacle.

An alternative, less well-trodden, path was chosen by one Erich Ledwinka, son of Hans, designer of the Czechoslovakian Tatra. Working at the Austrian company Steyr-Puch in the 1950s, Erich came up with the antithesis of the modern 4x4 – the little Haflinger. Named after a local breed of horse, the device was originally referred to as the 'Austrian Jeep,' although 'Mountain Goat' seemed more apt. Designed to carry four soldiers up any mountain, the occupants could also manhandle the vehicle.

The Haflinger was a beguiling mixture of simplicity, sophistication, and, one has to say, intelligence, it couldn't have been more different to the Land Rover's no-nonsense approach. If the British solution had a conventional car-like cab, the forward-control Austrian offering was unconventional in every respect.

Structure/mechanicals/body

The structure/body was based on a large backbone chassis/torque-tube containing a propeller shaft, mounted on each end of which were the differentials and gearbox. Pressed steel swinging arms with driveshafts inside pivoted off the differentials; these arms were then further located by radius struts angled back to the chassis/torque tube. The driveshafts/swinging arms were not fixed at the wheel hub centres, but some way above, because they indirectly drove the wheels through transfer gears, ie a portal axle. Mounted on top of the differentials were pressed steel cross arms, the ends of which were locating cups for the suspension's large diameter coil springs, with the bottom of the springs located on the hubs. Long stroke dampers were separate from the springs. This intriguing backbone chassis was just about all there was to the Haflinger.

The front assembly also carried the steering. Being a true forward-control vehicle, the driver and front passenger sat over the front wheels, and the protruding end of the steering column and linkage were way out in front of the chassis.

The engine hung out of the back, behind the rear axle line. It was a compact, 643cc, ducted, fan-cooled, flat-twin, developing 22bhp, later increased to 27bhp – an excellent unit, subsequently used in several other vehicle applications. Although gearing options were available, the 4x4's road speed was generally below 50mph.

Above the tubular backbone and mechanics was a flat platform with two seats and controls. The 'bodywork' consisted of a vestigial front cowling that protected the occupant's legs, and also carried the headlamps and folding windscreen. Two additional folding seats were stowed in footwells under trap doors in the rear. The rear-mounted engine lived in a protective box; spare wheel, fuel tank and additional stowage boxes were all under the flat floor, hanging down and visible. The rear deck often had side and tail boards to help with carrying loads and equipment.

THE STEYR-PUCH HAFLINGER WAS THE ANTITHESIS OF TODAY'S 4X4. LIGHT AND AGILE, WITH SUPERIOR GROUND CLEARANCE BESTOWED BY PORTAL AXLES, IT WAS DESIGNED TO CARRY FOUR SOLDIERS UP MOUNTAIN TRACKS.

Haflingers could have a partial or full canvas tilt, with side-screens for weather protection, but often the little device is seen stripped to the bare essentials with its windscreen folded flat.

The lack of superstructure gave a very low centre of gravity, which allowed quite extreme roll angles of 45 degrees, despite the narrow track required for mountain paths. Front and rear underbody were abruptly angled to accommodate maximum ramp angles. The unusually good ground clearance of 10.3in (262mm) was achieved by the portal axles, which lifted the potentially ground-fouling driveshafts and differentials much higher than you would expect for 12in (305mm) wheels.

The Haflinger could ford 14in (350mm) of water.

Most 4x4s achieve good ground clearance by using larger diameter wheels, but this also increases the weight and centre of gravity. Haflinger wheels had a generous 10in (254mm) of travel.

Both differentials could be locked so that, even if only one wheel had traction, the vehicle could proceed. Climbing ability was noted as a 41 degree angle, and, judging by footage of these vehicles, climbing ability and angles of operation depended not so much on the vehicle, but how creative/brave/mad the driver was.

The Haflinger weighed 1422lb (645kg) with 22bhp, while the smallest contemporary Series One Land Rover of

To Boldly Go

1958 weighed 2740lb (1243kg), and had 52bhp available.

So the Mountain Goat was roughly half the weight and power of a comparable Land Rover, and thus the two shared a not-dissimilar power-to-weight ratio. Given that weight is undesirable on mud and gradients, it's understandable that some off-road enthusiasts maintain that the Mountain Goat is a contender for the 'most capable of all 4x4s' title. Design is a compromise, however, and the conventional Solihull offering was, and is, more at ease on public roads.

How Haflingers were used in practice

Following the 1958 prototype, production began in 1959, when the Austrian and Swiss army bought Haflingers to replace the ageing Willys Jeep. Production ceased 16,647 units later, in 1975. It's thought about 7000 were employed by various armed forces, including the Royal Navy who used them for helicopter tugs and maintenance buggies, including some carrier based. The Australian army also had them. Able to carry 1102.3lb (500kg), and only 112.2in (2850mm) long and 55in (1400mm) wide, they were useful for general purpose support duties, radio-equipped command vehicles, rapid-response fire fighting and ambulances, etc, especially where terrain or access was difficult. Despite being small, they appealed to the military as mobile platforms for recoilless weapon systems. There were more than 30 variants including, later, fully-enclosed fibreglass cabins, and the tracked Schneewiesel (snow weasel). In Austria they were popular for hunting trips in the mountains.

From 1961, a fifth, gravity-defying, crawler gear was available. There was a comprehensive options list, including a side-mounted powered winch and associated ground anchor! One could imagine them as particularly suitable for afforestation work, operating miles off the beaten track in hilly terrain. Regardless of role, the basic structure remained unchanged with the 700AP standard 59in (1500mm) wheelbase, and the 703AP of 71in (1800mm) wheelbase.

In retrospect

The demise of these willing workhorses was primarily due to the growing strictures of regulations, including emissions, and market expectations of normal road use, more powerful engines, and air-conditioning, etc. But the legend abided, and Haflingers continued to be used, negotiating seemingly impossible mud, rock and gradient obstacles in Trial events to the delight of participants and spectators alike.

A lesson in minimalism and fulfilment of a tight design brief for any industrial design student, the modern 4x4 off-roaders are wonderfully capable machines, although the little Austrian mountain goat demonstrated that might is not always right.

In 1962 the Indonesian military purchased 1000 Haflingers, which must have made the Steyr-Puch concern very happy indeed.

Although the open road was not the Mountain Goat's natural habitat, long journeys were undertaken, and in 1983, one was driven from Vermont to California, and another 10,000 miles from Vienna to the tip of the Arabian Peninsula.

Such was the Haflinger's off-road ability that it even competed in televised rallycross-type events. Should it fall over, the driver could usually right it and carry on.

ARIEL SQUARE FOUR 'HOME BREW'

13

1960

'SPECIALS' USING A 1930S AUSTIN 7 OR FORD CHASSIS WERE THE FORERUNNERS OF THE KIT-CAR INDUSTRY. BASED ON 1930S SPORTS CAR STYLES, STEEL OR ALUMINIUM BODIES GRADUALLY GAVE WAY TO FIBREGLASS, WHICH SUITED SMALL PRODUCTION RUNS.

YOUNG ANTHONY GOULD BUILDS A SPECIAL THREE-WHEELER

Special. *Adj.* 1. distinguished from, set apart from, or excelling others of its kind. 2. designed or reserved for a particular purpose. 3. not usual or commonplace. (*Collins Concise Dictionary.*)

No account of vehicles that have appealed to enthusiasts over the years would be complete without touching on the phenomenon of the 'Special.'

Background to 'Specials'

Homemade cars have never been called homemade cars; in the UK at least, they are always referred to as Specials, and the people who build them Special builders. All industrialised countries have had some form of one-off vehicles, inevitably sporty, built by professionals, semi-professionals, and rank amateurs. The Americans have produced the greatest number of one-offs, but they call them Hot Rods or just Rods, and tend to combine 'show' and 'go' with some amazing creations, often favouring professional shops to do the work. The UK has a long and, some say, honourable tradition of one-offs, built by one-off types of people.

Motivation in the UK tended to be a combination of the desire for something racy (a two-seater open car, say), a lack of funds to buy such a beast, and a hard-to-explain urge to create something different – which certain Brits are susceptible to. Specials have always been built since motoring began, but the movement really took off in the late 1930s, continued well into the 1960s,

77

To Boldly Go

and never completely died out. The urge to build something original has now largely been satisfied by the kit car phenomenon, many examples of which started as Specials that worked well enough to justify selling a kit of parts for enthusiasts to build their own.

The 1939 formation of the 750 Motor Club was a key event, as Specials based on the 1922-1939 Austin 7 chassis could be involved in competition formulas. Apart from circuit racing, 'mud-plugging' hillclimbs and Trials events were especially popular. The roll of honour of constructors is a long one – Sir Alec Issigonis and Colin Chapman to name but two.

Anything with a separate chassis attracted the attention of Specials builders, but the Austin 7 with its simple 747cc side-valve engine, the 1932-37 Ford model Y, and the 1953 1172cc 100E Ford Popular (both side-valve), were natural candidates. Some of the older cars were practically valueless as the 1950s progressed, enabling Specials building components to be within reach of even the most hard-up enthusiast.

Construction and mechanicals of Specials

A 747cc, 993cc or 1172cc engine would breathe a sigh of relief when hundredweights of steel and glass were gleefully hacked off and thrown away. The running chassis could then have a new, lightweight, open two-seater body fashioned on it, although it's necessary to acknowledge that some of the new creations were aesthetically borderline. In the Austin 7's case, the factory and coachbuilders had been producing quite attractive two-seaters in the MG mould during the 1930s, and many aped these.

Newly released from heavy saloon bodies, and pepped-up by various degrees of tuning, a reasonable power-to-weight ratio could be achieved. Austin and Ford Specials created a lively market for performance equipment. Many firms were engaged in satisfying this specialised demand, ranging from leather bonnet straps, through to 'bolt-on' twin-carburettors, early alloy wheels, alloy cylinder heads, new brakes and suspension components, etc. Several companies sold fibreglass bodies, echoing the contemporary sports cars or coupés. This trend, of course, developed into today's kit car industry. The Lotus Seven/Caterham/Westfield, and countless similar models, owe their existence to the earlier Specials scene of pre- and postwar years.

The span of Specials design went from the basic Austin A-frame, or Ford chassis, with very rudimentary aluminium and plywood superstructures, to some quite sophisticated creations, assembled from chalk marks on the garage floor, to a semi-professional new chassis with a panel-beaten or fibreglass coupé body. Several period books were written on the subject, one of which shows an original Lotus Elite-type body with a new steel tube chassis: practically the only Austin 7 component retained was the engine block.*

The Gould Special

An intriguing stratum of Specials builders comprises those individuals who take the path less well-trodden, and, starting with a clean sheet of paper, try to gain some advantage over fellow competitors, or simply strive for a totally unique vehicle, whether for road or race. They regard building on an existing chassis to be too much of a compromise, and a good example of this is the hero of our story, Anthony Gould.

A young jig-maker apprentice in the late 1950s, who wanted some genuinely sporty transport, Gould had only one

G.H 13

ANTHONY GOULD'S 1960 THREE-WHEELER WAS SPECIAL ENOUGH FOR THE MOTOR CYCLE TO TEST IT. GOULD WAS A PIONEER OF JOINING A BIKE REAR TO A CAR FRONT: AN APPROACH THAT PROVED POPULAR INTO THE NEXT CENTURY.

option: motorbikes. If he wanted exciting motoring and couldn't stretch to a Morgan three-wheeler he was pretty much out of luck. In addition, I suspect our Anthony was cursed with that irritating itch, the urge to create.

Scratching the itch

So, aged 17, with virtually no funds, this apprentice began to assemble bits and pieces for his 'dream machine.' The rear end came from a scrapped Ariel Square Four motorbike, there were parts from the ubiquitous Austin 7, a fuel tank was fashioned from an oil drum, etc, etc, and the simple but effective formula of melding a motorbike rear end to a car-like front began to gel.

No doubt there are earlier examples of such a hybrid, but it was novel enough in February 1960 for the highly-respected magazine *The Motor Cycle* to feature it as a noteworthy one-off Special. It's worth mentioning that, over half a century later, several UK and USA companies produce devices using the same formula of

rear-half-bike, front-half-car, all of them notable for their more than adequate performance (understatement) in both speed and cornering ability. Examples are the BMW-powered Grinnall Scorpion, Yamaha-powered RTR, Hayabusa-powered Razor, and the USA's T-Rex – but there are many more.

Whilst not in today's super-bike league, the Ariel Square Four was regarded in its day as rather exotic. This 1938 four-cylinder, 997cc, air-cooled engine produced 45bhp in standard form, but, of course, in the best tradition, Anthony tuned it, raising the compression ratio from 5.9 to 7.2:1, by opening the ports, and replacing the Solex with a larger SU carburettor. A coil ignition replaced the magneto; there was a new exhaust system, and a starting-handle on an outrigger supplanted the kickstart.

The vehicle's dry weight was 5.5cwt (279.4kg), considerably less than the 8cwt (406.4kg) limit for cheaper three-wheeler road tax. Still under development

To Boldly Go

when *The Motor Cycle* magazine tested it, and 80mph was achieved – a little faster than most Morgans, and significantly faster than run-of-the-mill saloons. It could also be thrown around corners with an abandon certainly unwise in most postwar cars. Gould's efforts showed that wide tyres weren't essential if the vehicle's basics were right – something the just-launched Mini was beginning to demonstrate.

The skills and determination involved in building such a unique Special should not be underestimated: a space frame chassis, machining front hubs and stub axles, incorporating Austin 7 steering and Morris Eight hydraulic brakes, plus a handbrake for the rear. In addition, protecting the air-cooled engine buried in the rear from overheating was achieved by using air scoops and a large oil-cooler. To have it enthusiastically featured in the specialist press upon completion would have been praise indeed, and, for a

20-year-old, quite remarkable. No doubt Anthony observed later interpretations of his ideas with a satisfied smile.

The overall aesthetic of Gould's Special is no-nonsense and satisfactory: an example of form-follows-function, that even cheekily featured just a single headlamp as the minimum legal requirement. This creation is not pretty, but does convey the nature of a purposeful sports machine. Not trying to ape anyone else's style, it simply sits there and says 'Let's Go!'

Specials in retrospect

Automotive history provides rich pickings for anyone interested in sociology or what makes people tick. What we use as transport reflects on where we are at any point in time. Anyone familiar with 1930/40/50s illustrations depicting images of flying cars, personal jet-packs, and roads in the sky, might consider that many in the 21st century now

GOULD'S STEEL-TUBE FRAME ACCOMMODATED A MODIFIED 997cc ARIEL SQUARE FOUR MOTORBIKE REAR END. ONE-OFFS HAVE TO TACKLE ISSUES SUCH AS THE HANDBRAKE, CONVERTING A KICKSTART TO A STARTING HANDLE, ETC, ETC, ETC.

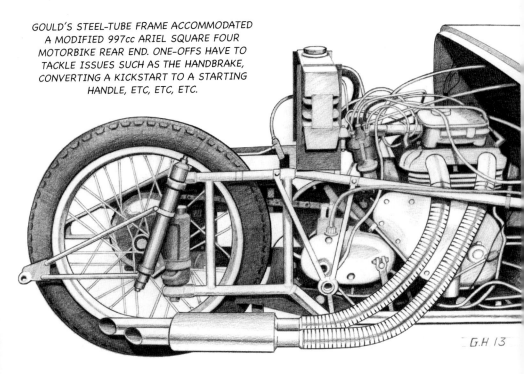

NO SLUGGARD, GOULD'S BREADLINE BLASTER WENT WELL ENOUGH FOR THE MOTOR CYCLE JOURNALIST TO GIVE THE PROJECT A GLOWING WRITE-UP.

regard a simple folding bicycle as a good method of city transport. People have a way of working round less-than-ideal circumstances. So it was with Specials builders: many young men, impatient for their dream machine to materialise, set about making their own from not much more than scrap. The resultant devices ranged from the 'I think I'll take the bus, thank you,' to the big smile on *The Motor Cycle* tester's face. Well done, our Tony!

* This ultimate Austin 7 Special was LM (Bill) Williams' LMW GT Coupé. Williams and Colin Chapman knew each other.

The Lotus Elite can be seen as a progression from one-off Specials philosophy to mainstream production commitment.

Some say that three-wheelers are a solution to a problem that doesn't exist. Well, I wish there were more people who could solve such 'problems' in the way Anthony Gould did in the late 1950s.

A period term for Specials, 'Bitza' (bits of this and bits of that) tended to be used for motorcycle home-builds.

Specials are always evocative of their time. One can imagine Anthony Gould working to resolve some issue in the workshop, with a mug of tea and the radio playing Buddy Holly, The Everly Brothers and Johnny Kidd and the Pirates. Earlier devotees doubtless listened to dance bands and swing. Happiness doesn't require a lot of money.

BMW RACING
SIDECARS

1960-1974

SIDECARS ATTRACT UNIQUE
PERSONALITIES, SUCH AS
HARD-CHARGING FLORIAN
CAMATHIAS ON HIS
BMW-POWERED KNEELER.
CAMATHIAS WAS KILLED AT
BRANDS HATCH IN 1965 WHEN
HIS FRONT FORKS FAILED.

CAMATHIAS, DEUBEL, ENDERS, FATH AND SCHEIDEGGER – THE DANGEROUS BALLET

Some motor cars and fellow travellers in the world of wheels are fascinating, but it invariably takes the human element to make them special in time and place. It's often the association with their creators or users that elevates a machine to a special place: the enthusiast's Shangri-la. This close relationship between man and machine is never more evident than that which exists between racing sidecar outfits and crews. To this scribe, that fusion became most potent in the 1960s, when the names Camathias, Deubel, Enders, Fath and Scheidegger became forever associated with the dangerous ballet that is sidecar racing.

Background

No account of the wilder aspects of competition machines would be complete without broaching the subject of sidecars. People have raced everything from penny-farthings to trucks, both of which are more sensible than sidecar outfits. I mean, you take a motorcycle, and, using a scaffolding of steel tubes, bolt a one-wheeled carriage alongside it for a passenger!

Structurally and dynamically everything is wrong. Motorcycle wheels and suspension aren't designed to take sideways loads, the host bike generally wants to turn towards its parasitic burden, braking is asymmetric, even assuming the outrigger wheel has a brake (which it usually didn't), the engine/gearing isn't intended to pull such a load, and the device's layout favours either left- or right-hand bends, depending on which side the 'chair' is.

Sidecar men employ all sorts of strategies to compensate for this unnatural coupling. Toe-in the outrigger wheel slightly to compensate for sidecar drag, and lean the bike out slightly to compensate for road camber, before tightening all the bolts. Change the front forks, wheels, tyres, springs, dampers, brakes and gearing ... get the picture?

Necessity is the mother of invention, of course, and, in the 1920s and 1930s, motorcyclists with wives and then children welcomed this apparently simple solution to their transport needs. Indeed, by 1939, 30% of all motorcycles were combinations. Remove the domestic necessity, and what's the logic of racing such a contrivance? But then, why race anything (see earlier reference to penny-farthings and trucks)?

The instant appeal of sidecar racing is the enthusiastic/desperate efforts of the crew to coax the contraption round bends without capsizing, whilst also endeavouring to keep the device pointing in the right direction under, usually violent, braking and acceleration. The occupants are a gymnastic double-act, as, working in unison, they throw their weight from left to right in a crowd-pleasing, thrilling display. One moment the dynamic duo are trying to make themselves aerodynamically invisible; the next, the passenger is hanging out like a dinghy sailor, or leaning over the rear wheel for balance and added traction.

Racing outfits evolved over the years

from the simplest bolt-on approach, through extensive dustbin fairings, to the sophisticated asymmetric three-wheeled 'racing cars' of today. In a case of evolution denied, this later trend resulted in the passenger being no more than a 'sack of potatoes' ballast, such was the vehicle's stability. The governing body quite reasonably felt that the crowd-pleasing (and money-making) heroics of the passenger were lost as a result, so the dial was turned back a few clicks, and regulations stipulated that the passenger had to be able to move around an open platform, and the rider/driver must use handlebars, and not a steering wheel!

Mechanical and structural

This chapter revolves around a group of sidecar men, and one engine: the legendary, even mystical, BMW Rennsport RS 54, which was one of the first production racing motorcycles to emerge from postwar Germany in 1954.

As a solo machine, its handling was felt to be less than ideal – even unstable – but the bike's flat-twin engine was perfect for sidecar racing. In 1955, one Wilhelm Noll set an absolute world speed sidecar record of 174.1mph, with a fully enclosed streamline bike with an outrigger wheel (124mph is mentioned regarding an unfaired solo). The 493.9cc horizontally opposed, air-cooled, flat-twin 'Boxer-Engine' produced about 45-50bhp. It had gear-driven, twin overhead camshafts on each cylinder.

Originally a long-stroke engine, over 20 years of racing development, the RS engine evolved into a short-stroke unit, with typically 10.5:1 compression ratio, a 38mm Dell'Ortos carburettor for each cylinder, and many slight improvements, eventually producing about 64bhp. By 1972 maximum speed for the BMW outfits is quoted as 135mph.

It is regarded by all as a very special

power unit, and described as 'old-world craftsmanship and new wave technology.' It is thought a maximum of 50 were built, which were used and reused in numerous machines. The power unit proved so successful in sidecars that, in 1958, BMW stopped supporting the solos. The horizontally-opposed flat- twin was ideal for the job with the two cylinders obviously much lower than on the usual vertical engines. The rider/driver probably gained some small comfort from the fact that an engine blow-up might tend to send debris sideways rather than vertically, with the passenger having a 50/50 chance of benefiting.

BMW was unique amongst its contemporaries in using a shaft-drive, ie bevel gears, rather than a chain and sprocket for transmitting power to the rear wheel. Rear suspension was dual swinging-arm, with the driveshaft inside the right-hand arm. Front suspension abandoned telescopic forks in favour of Earles-type forks, built under licence from Englishman Ernie Earles. This was a robust, twin leading-arm arrangement, whose geometry and action was better suited to the sideways loads imposed by a sidecar.

Given an apparently ideal engine, the main thrust of development for BMW outfits was chassis and aerodynamics. During the formula's evolution, the step change was the 'semi-kneeler' or 'kneeler' by Brits Eric Oliver in 1953 and Ernie Earles in 1954. Up until this period the rider was still sitting *on* the machine with the fuel tank under his chest. By taking away the fuel tank, the rider could be positioned considerably lower, actually supported on his knees and wrists (thus kneeling). The fuel tank or tanks were accommodated anywhere else possible on the outfit – usually in the middle at the back. Smaller wheels were used to reduce height, but continued to be traditional motorcycle wire-spokes, until car-type alloy wheels were favoured towards the end of the 1960s.

Obviously, the lower the outfit and occupants, the lower the centre of gravity for road holding, and accompanying reduced frontal area for wind resistance.

By the late 1950s, German machines began adopting the 'kneeler.' Dustbin fairings and streamlined windscreens were all intended to aid aerodynamics. The BMW cycle frame, like its competitors, morphed into a space-frame structure integrating the passenger platform. Like any racing machine, all elements were as light as possible.

Apart from the memorable sound of the power unit's flat bark, the lasting impression when seeing these BMW machines is just how compact and neat they are.

Man and machine

The 1960s and early 1970s saw a golden age of sidecar racing, as men and machine reached a level of spectacle perhaps since equalled, but never bettered. The names of several legendary and heroic charioteers echo across the years, their common denominator being the BMW twin-cylinder boxer engine.

Florian Camathias

Numerous anecdotes, some possibly true, abound about this man from Switzerland, due to his myopic vision, such as going to bed in the wrong room at his Isle of Man accommodation. A determined opponent to Max Deubel, Camathias often pushed his machine to the limit and beyond, until he was killed at Brands Hatch in 1965 when the new lightweight front forks failed on his kneeler.

Max Deubel

A German who was World Champion in 1961, 1962, 1963 and 1964, with passenger Emil Horner. That sort of successful run is witness to a highly talented rider and a very well prepared machine. Although trying a kneeler, he was happier on low 'sitter/squatter' outfits. In the 1966 Isle of Man Sidecar TT, Deubel achieved the first over-90mph lap. He retired in 1966 to run his hotel.

Klaus Enders

A German who was World Champion in 1967, 1969, 1970, 1972, 1973 and 1974. In the 1969 Isle of Man Sidecar TT, Enders achieved a new lap record of 92.54mph. With passenger Ralf Engelhardt, he had an extraordinary run of six championships, again proving the supremacy of the BMW sidecars powered by the RS 54. He was the last of the BMW World Champions; for the next two years the complex multi-cylinder Konigs won, then followed the many successes of

exotic Yamaha-powered machines. Enders retired after his last successful season.

Helmut Fath

A German who used the BMW engine to secure the 1960 World Championship. It seems that, following an accident, BMW wouldn't support his efforts, so, being a gifted engineer, Fath built his own four-cylinder URS engines to win the championship again in 1968. He retired in 1969.

Fritz Scheidegger

Also from Switzerland, Scheidegger was World Champion in 1965 and 1966 (on a true kneeler), but was killed at Mallory Park in 1967, when, it was reported, a rear chassis component failed. His World Championship passenger, Briton John Robinson, survived the accident, but retired from the sport.

THERE ARE NO OTHER FORMS OF MOTORSPORT WHERE MEN AND MACHINE ARE MORE CLOSELY COMBINED. HERE, GERMAN SIDECAR MASTER MAX DEUBEL LEADS SWISS-BORN FLORIAN CAMATHIAS. BOTH USED THE BMW RENNSPORT RS 54 ENGINE.

To Boldly Go

Considering the pressure cooker of competition developments, it's extraordinary that, for 20 years, the same engine powered these riders, and others, to victory, and was responsible for some remarkable results in the book of records.

Summary

The BMW outfits were compact, efficient, and even elegant machines, arguably representing the high water mark of genuine motorcycle/sidecar outfits, as they were mainly constructed of steel tubing, and used two-cylinder air-cooled engines.

The BMW RS54s were characterised by the exhaust's evocative flat bark, and the cylinder barrels and heads sticking out each side for cooling, with their large carburettors and intake trumpets. Somehow, these white machines looked as though nature had intended them this way.

In the early 1970s, monocoque structures completely melded bike and chair components, and multi-cylinder, water-cooled, car-type engines became the norm. Today's racing sidecars remain fascinating solutions to a dynamic quandary, that continues as quirky, even eccentric, to say the least, but the human acrobatic component still creates one of the most thrilling spectacles that motorsport has to offer.

To a certain generation the exotic-sounding, foreign names of those racing an obviously effective machine created a time and legend that lives on: Camathias, Deubel, Enders, Fath, and Scheidegger, masters of those unlikely machines, as they performed their riveting but dangerous ballet. Overall, this unlikely sport encapsulates the spirit of creative enthusiasts pushing the boundaries of design and technology in the quest for performance.

Chris Vincent, in the early 1960s, briefly succeeded in challenging BMW supremacy. Compensating for less-than-ideal BSA 500 and 650cc engines, he built a very low outfit, whose excellent handling was a revelation in the traditional world of sidecar wrestling. The Continentals soon copied his design principles.

Harry Carpenter*, the well known BBC sports reporter, specialised in rather over-excited boxing commentary. A slight cut on a pugilist would have Carpenter exclaiming that there was 'blood everywhere,' and that the fight 'couldn't go on.' Some humorist decided he should be passenger to 1977 sidecar World Champion George O'Dell, and so, wearing racing leathers and a microphone, Harry set off around a racing circuit with George.

Carpenter immediately launched into his trademark, over-the-top, highly excitable description about the incredible acceleration and cornering forces, etc. It was apparent from the revs that George was actually taking it fairly steadily, but, as these increased, so, too, did Carpenter's voice, until it eventually became an incoherent shriek.

---

* Forever associated with heavyweight champion Frank Bruno's "Know what I mean, 'arry," followed by a rumbling chuckle.

At one event, as the outfits battled to out-drag each other away from the grid, one passenger lost his grip and cartwheeled off the back. His determinedly focused pilot didn't realise anything was amiss until the first bend ...

On the opening lap of a historic sidecar race at Oulton Park, the three front runners all took an 'escape road' (Fosters circuit) together, because no one was prepared to back off for the tight left-hander of Cascades.

PANHARD 24CT

1963-1967

PANHARD 24CT'S STYLING IS OUTSTANDING. THE LOW FRONT, WRAP-AROUND BUMPER, MINIMUM AIR-INTAKE, AND HEADLAMP TREATMENT WAS AN INFLUENTIAL NEW DIRECTION.

GH13

"SEUL L'EXPERIENCE LE PLUS ANCIENNE PERMET LES SOLUTIONS LES PLUS MODERNES"*

It's said that Citroën draughtsmen had to present their work to an inspector, who, if he'd seen anything like it before, tore up the drawing. Maybe it's something in the grapes, but Panhard apparently employed this chap's brother.

Background

Panhard made its first vehicles in 1891. Its last vehicle, the 24CT, ceased production in 1967, having previously been absorbed by Citroën. Although known since the Second World War for avant-garde engineering, pre-1939, it had made cars mechanically typical of their day, sometimes indulging in frankly bizarre art nouveau styling.

1950-1960s mechanicals & body

Panhard, realising in the late 1940s that economy and efficiency would be required, designed an air-cooled, horizontally opposed, 610cc flat-twin engine. Front-wheel drive and, due to local availability, all-aluminium body construction were adopted. By 1954 it had arrived at its idiosyncratic Dyna Z Panhard, a 15ft (4572mm) long four-door sedan, weighing 14cwt (711.2kg) unladen. By now the flat-twin was 850cc, and developing 42bhp at 5000rpm, in a vehicle capable of 75mph, averaging 34mpg, and a six-seater! In 1959, the Dyna Z was face-lifted into the PL17, able to cruise at 80mph, and achieving 50mpg at 50mph. A steel body increased weight to 16.5cwt (838kg).

The alloy engine had a shrouded-turbine cooling system, a patented cageless, roller-bearing big-end with small rollers separating load-bearing large rollers. Cylinder heads were integral with the cylinder barrels, and the pushrod-operated valve-train used torsion bars instead of coil springs.

Flat-twins encourage sustained high revs as they smooth out at speed, and the Panhard engine was designed with this in mind. This 850cc engine was recognised as highly effective, and many French specials and competition cars used it. In 1961, PL17s came first, second and third in the Monte Carlo Rally; also winning the up-to-1000cc class in previous years.

The wheel hubs/brake drums were unusual, the latter being finned alloy castings that protruded through the 14in (355mm) wheels, the rim of which was

then bolted on to the drum's periphery, avoiding the need to draw brake-cooling air through the wheel (see also Steyr Puch 650TR). Suspension was also unconventional, with the front hubs located at the end of two upper and lower transverse leaf springs. The rear was just as intriguing, with a rigid fixed 'axle,' from the ends of which trailing arms were pivoted, sprung by three transverse torsion bars each side. The hubs were further located by diagonal struts pivoted in the centre of the fixed axle; rubber cushions were located above the hubs.

Aerodynamics

Pre-1940s 'streamlining' influenced car shapes, but the scientific approach of

PANHARD'S 1963 SVELTE, SOPHISTICATED, 24CT COUPÉ'S REAR THREE-QUARTER ASPECT, WITH ITS SLIM TAPERED TAIL, WAS AESTHETIC PERFECTION. THE 'FLOATING' ROOF PANEL REDUCES VISUAL WEIGHT; EARLY CARS FEATURED POLISHED CAST-ALLOY BRAKE DRUMS.

developing car bodies in wind tunnels was arguably the last major influence on car shapes. The 1967 NSU Ro80 (coefficient of drag, Cd 0.355), 1982 Ford Sierra (Cd 0.34) and 1982 Audi 100 (Cd 0.3) were all styled with wind tunnel feedback as a prime driver, when contemporaries were Cd 0.4+.

Since 2000, styling design has been increasingly steered by degrees of marketing and brand identity body language. That's not to say there aren't, or won't be, exciting and creative automotive forms, but one is talking of nuance rather than step-change.

None had taken aerodynamics more seriously than Panhard which, with its 1949 Dynavia concept car's tear-drop shape (Cd 0.26), influenced the Citroën DS (1964 Cd 0.33), it's argued. It's not possible to discuss postwar Panhards without mentioning airflow management. Louis Bionier, head of the body design department, was fascinated by the dynamics of birds and fishes. He extensively used wind tunnels at St Cyr and Laboratoire Eiffel. 1954 Dyna Z models had been finessed to Cd O.236; however, production cars have to live in the real world of air-intakes, gutters, windscreen wipers and body gaps, etc, and the Dyna Z on the road was in the respectable area between Cd O.34 and Cd O.35.

The Panhard Dyna Z is an overt, almost cartoon-like, low-drag shape. No hard edge is presented to the airflow, either straight

GH.13

ahead or in yaw, where the air meets the vehicle obliquely. The compact engine allows a low front end, and the ducted air-cooling doesn't require a large opening for a radiator matrix. Its style is 'in-the-round,' avoiding turbulence-inducing features, and regarded now as an archetypical 1950s aerodynamic shape. The slightly florid details of the face-lifted Dyna Z, the PL17, degraded the Cd somewhat.

The culmination of Louis Bionier's striving – and resistance of marketing's siren song of visual embellishments – resulted in the 1963 24CT's Cd 0.34; again, early models were perhaps in the Cd 0.2 area. Maybe Panhard was forced into aerodynamic pioneering by the 850cc power source, but the economy and top speeds show how successful it was.

What wasn't fully understood at this time was the critical nature of rear airflow on drag and directional stability. Generally, even if you have the length for a tear-drop tail, it's better to chop it off abruptly, and/or make sure the middle of the boot or rear decking has an airflow break-away high point (largely now universal). Even in recent years, rear end stability issues have only been recognised when a representative prototype is tested on the road – witness the late addition of a fence spoiler on the original Audi TT's boot. The Ford Sierra, which was extensively flow tested, still required rear end fine tuning when in production.

Aerodynamics aren't simple (witness F1 cars) but Panhard was an acknowledged pioneer in its day.

Index of Performance – Le Mans

The efficient 850cc engine, coupled with aerodynamic knowledge, led to low drag, fuel efficient, and fast Le Mans cars, which (some say relentlessly) won the Index of Performance category in the 1950s and early 1960s. This was a valid test of performance and

fuel consumption, culminating in the extraordinary Charles Deutsch CD LM 64 – an aerodyne teardrop with enclosed wheels and a quoted Cd of 0.12. Proving that low drag isn't the whole answer, on its long low tail stood tall twin fins for high speed stability. Mind you, with its five-speed gearbox, this supercharged 850cc was timed at 140mph!

Panhard 24CT & 24B (CT – Coupé Touristique)

Having delved into Panhard's history and design philosophy, we can better understand and appreciate its finest hour: the 24CT. The preceding Dyna Z/PL17 sedan is an exceptional design, both mechanically and aesthetically, and, being recognised as such, has been exhibited in the London Design Museum. So, just how good does it get when you take a shortened PL17 platform and dress it in a coupé body that this devotee still regards as an all-time great?

24CT body/styling

Coupés, particularly 2+2s, have one principal aim in life: to look so desirable that people ignore any shortcomings, such as inadequate rear head- and legroom, mediocre performance, oh, and long doors for rear passenger ingress and egress, causing parking aggravation.

A good example of the genre was the 1989 Vauxhall Calibre (Cd 0.26), a seductive coupé that caused sales reps to go weak at the knees with automotive lust.

When launched there was nothing else like the 24CT. The visual impact of the low, unbroken wrap-around front, with faired-in headlamps, was in a class of its own: a degree of aesthetic sophistication 20 years ahead of its time.

The 14ft (4276mm) long, low and sleek coupé was original from stem to stern. The twin headlamps behind glass were hypnotic, the complete lack of any conventional radiator or obvious air intake ensured nothing detracted from those 'eyes,' and the wrap-around polished bumpers underlined the headlamps.

The front was so compelling, one didn't realise how daring the waist's wide, shoulder-ledge joining the front wings to the rear wings actually was. Beneath the bold waistline, panels were scalloped or hollowed. This unusual sculpturing of the doors and wings (see Marlene Dietrich's cheekbones) reduced visual weight, whilst stiffening the pressings and making the car look longer.

Perhaps the cleverest element was the unique 'floating roof' – this body-coloured panel was very flat, and supported by large glass areas and polished metal pillars. Launch cars had silver-painted roofs, which emphasised this separate superstructure floating above the slinky body. Interesting to note that even adventurous Panhard was restricted to flat side-glass.

Like many head-turning styles, the 24CT was not very space efficient: anything other than box-shaped wastes volume. This coupé ate into volume by running the strong-shouldered waistline from front to back, forcing the flat side-glass inboard conversely, though this reduced frontal area, improving aerodynamic drag. The steeply-raked windscreen and backlight also reduced cabin space.

'Squared-up' wheel cut-outs and subtle eyebrows further enhanced vehicle length. The scalloped side-section continued and deepened across the rear, with slim, wrap-around tail lamps. A bright strip ran around the car's lower waist, stopping only on the front wing to point at those compelling 'eyes.' The quirky, out-of-phase, clap-hand windscreen wipers added to the allure and mystique.

By its c1958 conception, Panhard was using all the black arts gleaned in the wind tunnel to craft this advanced form. In its final iteration the 850cc, 60bhp Tigre engine could (given a long enough road) take this svelte coupé to 100mph. With this sort of performance, the exotic, finned alloy brake drums were replaced by disc brakes requiring conventional ventilated wheels.

Steel body panels bolted on to a steel monocoque, and were removable, as on the Citroën DS and Rover 2000. Easy to build and repair, this construction avoided toxic lead-loaded joints. The large pressings that formed the front of the car forward of the windscreen had a conventional opening bonnet, but for major work the entire front body hinged.

Interior
The interior was better than the period's norm, with clean lines and detail typical of, say, Pininfarina. Large leather-trimmed, multi-adjustable seats were impressive. A complex heater ducting system even attempted to get hot air to the backlight. Restrained elegant interior sophistication echoed that of the exterior; students of design should look at late versions of Panhard's PL17 futuristic fascia, pure '60s, *Eagle* comic's Dan Dare.

Styling conclusion
From a styling/design perspective, one would have to have a heart of stone not to appreciate the conceptual imagination and masterly execution of the 24CT. Borrowing from little that went before (though some spoilsports cite the 1960 Chevrolet Corvair), one needs only to imagine this Panhard surrounded by typical late 1950s cars to realise how futuristic it was – a design masterclass.

On the road
Coupés don't necessarily have to major on

outright performance, which, in the 24CT's case, is just as well. Its steel body weighed 16.25cwt (825.5kg) – very apparent as you pull away with the two-cylinder engine working hard, and sounding agricultural, frankly. Trying to out-drag even average cars is pretty pointless and somewhat embarrassing; the analogy that comes to mind is a marathon runner attempting a sprint.

On the open road it becomes clear that typical French open country is its natural habitat. It is very good at fast cruising: the previously intrusive noise of the engine settles down to a contented hum; there is little wind noise, and the good size wheels, excellent suspension and comfortable seats work well together. Cornering is flat and reassuring. All-round visibility is excellent.

Travelling in the 24CT provides a sense of occasion: it's hard to explain but it just *feels* special. Of course, it helps if you are besotted by its styling, like this observer who refuses to hear a word against this charming, enigmatic French beauty.

Summary

When the PL17 ceased production in 1964, a stretched 24CT was put on the standard length PL17 platform and called the 24B or 24BT (if it used the Tigre engine), thus creating a genuine four-seater which retained its elegance.

Once fully under Citroën's control in 1965, Panhard's days were numbered. The jealous DS Goddess copied the 24's 'eye make-up,' as did many others. Toyota's mid-1980s Celica coupé acknowledged it borrowed from the 24CT's superstructure. Citroën did consider ways of keeping the coupé's beautiful body – a shortened DS platform was tried with either the 124bhp engine or a new twin-cam, 2-litre engine of 145bhp. With the twin-cam and five-speed gearbox it was capable of over 120mph, so a front spoiler was added; also slightly flared sills and exit air vents behind the front wheelarch.

The exercise was successful, but Citroën decided to build the 1970 SM instead. It also built a Maserati-powered 24CT with SM elements to test high-powered, front-wheel drive cars.

It's a tease that the 24CT's shape could have transferred to a high-performance Citroën DS platform, but maybe it's best to leave ghosts undisturbed ...

---

*Translation: "Only the oldest experience allows the most modern solutions." (Quote from Panhard publicity material.)

In 1963 in the UK, the 24CT cost £1400, the Jaguar Mk11 £1348, and the E-Type £1829: not a great prospect for a two-cylinder car which was also in the middle of the Citroën ID/DS price range.

Louis Bionier obviously had a good grasp of how to avoid aerodynamic drag; he was involved with the 1967 Citroën Dyane that was, in practice, at least 10mph faster than the Citroën 2CV (Cd 0.51), whose platform it used. The Dyane also inherited the 24CT's 'Dietrich' lower door section.

Manufacturers dissect and cost competitors' cars (Ford concluded early Minis were profitless). Investigating aluminium monocoques in the late '70s and early '80s, British Leyland and Audi obtained Panhard Dyna Zs, also wind tunnel testing them. A senior Rolls-Royce engineer personally ran one.

STEYR-PUCH 650TR

16

1964-1969

G.HULL 03

"AUSTRIA'S LITTLE BOMB" (*AUTOSPORT* MAGAZINE)

Automotive evolution occasionally throws up a surprise or aberration that makes life just a little bit more interesting; such is the strange case of the Steyr-Puch 'Fiat 500.'

Background

There has, of course, always been a tradition for go-faster Fiat 500s, the most famous and collectable being those modified by the Austrian-born Carlo Abarth. Surprisingly, the Italian companies were all outgunned by another Austrian source. Steyr-Daimler-Puch had previously achieved fame with its Haflinger 4x4, a mountain goat of a vehicle. Graduating to cars, and avoiding bodyshell tooling costs, it produced a novel hybrid: a cocktail of an imported Fiat 500 body with home-brewed mechanics.

Mechanicals

The Haflinger's horizontally-opposed flat-twin replaced the rather primitive Italian in-line vertical twin. There were various versions of this engine, but the one that interests us is the 660cc unit, powering the vehicle ultimately known as the Steyr-Puch 650TR II. It sported alloy cylinder heads, hemispherical combustion chambers, 10.5:1 compression ratio, hollow inlet-valves and sodium-filled exhaust valves, twin-choke carburettor, high-lift camshaft, lightened cam-followers, lightened flywheel and performance exhaust. If this did not whet your appetite, there was also a 'Monte Carlo' exhaust option, close ratio gears, and choice of final drive ratios.

The engine developed 39.5bhp at

93

To Boldly Go

POLISH WIZARD SOBIESLAW ZASADA CAMPAIGNED THE LITTLE 650TR PROJECTILE SUCCESSFULLY IN INTERNATIONAL RALLYING, PROVING THAT POWER-TO-WEIGHT RATIO AND 'CHUCK-ABILITY' CAN BETTER BRAWN.

5800rpm, and red-lined at 7000. The vehicle weighed just 9.8cwt (499kg), and 'standard' top speed was 87mph. A Bosch dynastart dynamo and starter were mounted behind a large ducted fan, connected to the engine crankshaft by impressive-looking twin belt pulleys. Pretty well the only Italian mechanicals were the steering and front transverse leaf-spring, further located by a Panhard rod. Large, powerful alloy brake drums, unique to Steyr, protruded through the wheel for cooling; the wheel rim was then bolted to the outside flange of the drum, as on the Panhard 24CT.

The rear suspension was swinging-arm with noticeable negative camber; the coil springs were supplemented by rubber compression units.

In the right hands, the car could rattle the heavier 998cc Mini-Cooper, and not be a pushover for the Cooper S. Interestingly, there was no common ground between the Austrian and British mechanical layouts at all.

Body

Although UK imports had the standard Fiat 500 roof with opening fabric panel, Steyr previously fitted its own full metal roof, incorporating a trailing-edge aerodynamic extension, similar to those in vogue today. Early versions had the original Fiat rear-hinged doors.

From the rear the only give-away for this 'Q' car were four large, horizontal air vents across the boot lid, but everyone assumed it was the harmless Italian clockwork mouse, anyway. Certainly, the Steyr-Puch had all the charm and style of the Fiat, and shared its surprising capacious interior space, excellent fields of vision and manoeuvrability. Visually, the Italians had arguably achieved the most perfect-looking small car ever!

What happened next – Sobiesław Zasada did!

The Steyr-Puch would have remained just a local Austrian tipple if the company had not decided to rally it. The driver it chose was Poland's Sobiesław

94

'Sobek' Zasada. Campaigning started in 1964 when, in the Polish round of the European Rally Championship, Zasada's 650TR won, with Eric Carlsson 2nd and Pat Moss 3rd. In 1965, out of 58 international rallies, Steyr-Puch finished first on ten occasions, and was winner in class 46 times. Zasada was 17th in the Monte Carlo Rally, 9th in the Tulip, 7th in the Acropolis, and 3rd in the

Geneva. He achieved 2nd in the Polish Rally, to Rauno Aaltonen in a Works Cooper S, and 3rd in the 1965 European Championship, behind Aaltonen and Trautmann, having also competed in the RAC Rally.

In 1966, the European Rally Championship was divided into Groups 1, 2 and 3. The 650TR was underpowered against Group 2 opposition, however

To Boldly Go

Zasada felt he had a chance, and did well, his main challenger being Timo Makinen's Cooper S. The championship hung on the RAC Rally.

According to *Motoring News*, Zasada had previously felt uncompetitive in this event, so chose not to enter, believing Makinen would break his own car. Makinen did just that, and Zasada won the 1966 Group 2 Championship. Steyr-Daimler-Puch had achieved more than it dared hope, but then gave up rallying, citing the high cost as the reason.

The author has subsequently chatted to a German engineer who was involved in circuit racing a 650TR at club level. On full song with 'Monte Carlo' exhaust, 4.87:1 final drive and straight-cut gears, it sounded like a big twin racing motorcycle, and was capable of very fast cornering with a 'hint' of oversteer.

Zasada was immediately offered a Porsche works drive in the team with Vic Elford, winning the 1967 European Rally Championship in Group 1 in a 912. Driving a BMW 2002 TI, he won the 1971 Championship. In all, he was three times European Rally Champion (1966, 1967 and 1971), and runner-up in 1968, 1969 and 1972. He was works driver for Steyr-Puch for three years, Porsche five years, BMW two years, and Mercedes three years.

By any standards, Sobiesław Zasada was obviously an exceptional driver, and perhaps no one else could have taken the 650TR to such heights. Contemporary reports don't appear to mention much in the way of mechanical trouble, except for a brake failure, a rare crash, and some tyre problems, which, considering the extreme circumstances, says a lot for the vehicle. On the Acropolis Rally, others joked that the potholes were bigger than the car! The tiny red projectile, with its nose buried beneath huge spotlamps, raucous exhaust and gear whine, had been quite a spectacle. Power was near to 50bhp, and top speed was about 95mph.

Testimony

In 1966, the company brochure and various road tests made heady reading, but, in this commentator's student world, it was a rich man's toy at £699.

Four years later, a dealer on the south coast had a 650TR traded-in. Its glory days long forgotten, the dealer didn't really know what it was, and my low offer for it was accepted.

FFX 2D was used for the M1/A5/M6 journey between London and Cheshire for some time. What Sir Henry Royce and WO Bentley would have said, if they had seen it parked outside the Rolls-Royce Apprentice Hostel at Crewe, does not bear thinking about, especially when the high compression ratio, on very cold mornings, demanded removal of a sparkplug to get it to spin fast enough to start on one barrel.

Driving the pocket rocket was quite an experience. With its short wheelbase and rear engine it had little real commitment to straight line travel, and if oversteer and tight bends were your cup of tea, it was great fun. It was more involving approaching 90mph in the Steyr-Puch than 150mph in a Mercedes S class on the Autobahn. The joke about an audio speedometer came to mind, "Saint Christopher speaking, 85mph and I'm out of here." Knock-knock-knocking on Heaven's door.

A weak-minded individual could use the surprising turn of speed to humiliate those dismissing the Steyr as a Fiat 500, and only the morally strong could resist this temptation. Once you forgot about trying to be a rally driver, the 650TR was a delight.

The horizontally-opposed engine was a little gem. It sat rather nose-high, so the front leaf spring was flattened, both for appearance and to prevent air getting under the front. It always felt better with passengers on board – certainly riding more smoothly – and even fully-loaded very little performance was sacrificed. An added bonus was that passengers acted as additional sound-deadening. The twin-choke Zenith would deliver 25-50mpg, depending on your self-control.

With hindsight, the car was a salutary reminder that great drivers really are a different breed. Zasada went straight from barely 50bhp with the Steyr-Puch, to 185bhp in a Group 3 911S. In his first rally he finished immediately behind Vic ('Quick Vic') Elford's Porsche.

Zasada, apart from anything else, must have had lightening-quick reflexes. Pushing your luck on a wet surface the 650TR could bite you; the transition between feeling generally in control and generally not was frighteningly sudden. Of course, being so light, the car could be collected quickly, but to exploit that hour after hour, flat-out on indifferent surfaces, would need extraordinary ability and talent. Achieving what he

did with the Steyr-Puch must remain one of the Polish Maestro's greatest rallying performances, and in motorsport generally, in fact. Now virtually forgotten, it would be nice to think of a 650TR in a collection somewhere, with a description of its achievements in the 1960s, witness to a special driver/machine combination. Whatever Zasada was paid, it could never have been enough.

A shameful conclusion

As regards FFX 2D, this chicken-hearted driver's nerve finally cracked one wild, wet and windy 1970s night on the M6's Staffordshire border. So violent were the gusts there was no choice but to drop into the lorry grooves on the inside lane. Even at 30mph, it was more like sailing a dingy. The car was traded in to a Cheshire dealer, who was left puzzling on his forecourt over the pronunciation of Steyr-Puch: he was convinced the car was a Fiat 500! Driving away in a Mini Cooper, the game little car's arch rival, seemed like an act of cruel betrayal.

Headline by Ronald Barker in *CAR* magazine, December 1966: "You Steyr – I'll Puch!"

Minding my business in the M1's centre lane, a well-preserved Triumph Stag cruised up behind me. The cloth-capped, string-back-gloved driver had a condescending smile as he flashed his headlamps to move me over. Finding a gap I duly got out of his way. I'd like to say I resisted the temptation to wind up the little red Austrian car, and go Stag hunting, but I'm only human.

GREENWOOD MINI

1965-1967

OWEN GREENWOOD'S RADICAL DESIGN WAS REGARDED BY MANY AS WILFULLY PROVOCATIVE.

G.H.13

"WELL, THAT'S NOT FAIR!"

Motorsport has one slightly regrettable but accepted constant – cheating. Okay, perhaps not actual cheating, but poring over regulations looking for loopholes, or an opportunity to gain advantage over fellow competitors, who, in turn, are also poring. As the stakes get higher, so a tiny, subtle advantage can often deliver significant returns. Formula 1 is the ultimate battleground for this. No season goes by without some team stealing a march; the exposed loophole then has to be sealed off or allowed for all. Witness Formula 1's 2010 'adjustable aerodynamics' controversy: regulations stipulated that no exterior part of the vehicle's body could be adjusted in motion, but McLaren (then Ferrari) realised air could be ducted through the cockpit, and the driver influence airflow to the rear aerofoils by moving his body – a cunning if underhand tactic.* Owen Greenwood, a seasoned sidecar racer in the 1960s, discovered a loophole so big he was able to drive a horse and cart through it: well, his 'cycle-car,' anyway.

Background

Owen Greenwood was typical of the self-funded privateer enthusiast who forms the backbone of motorsport. Working in a motorcycle dealership, he began competing in speedway and grass track racing at the age of 16. He was successful, but found that success at such a young age brought pressures he didn't enjoy, so briefly gave up.

Competition was in his blood, however, and he was soon drawn in again – this time to road racing. Using

BSA Gold Stars, and later a borrowed AJS 7R, Greenwood competed once a year at the Isle of Man Manx Grand Prix, and did reasonably well. A workmate, and sometime sidecar passenger, Terry Fairbrother, convinced Owen he'd enjoy racing sidecar outfits, and, thus, our story begins.

Not being financially over-endowed, Owen built several shoestring budget outfits, starting with a Norton featherbed frame, old Speedway 500cc JAP engine, and homemade sidecar chassis. In 1955, he was also racing a 500cc Manx Norton solo, subsequently fitting the engine into his sidecar. Triumph Tiger 100 and 110 engines also attracted his attention, and he even experimented with siamese Triumph Twins, creating a 1000cc, four-cylinder unit.

Between 1958 and 1964, Owen raced in around 30 events each season. In 1959 he finished sixth in the sidecar TT; the five outfits in front of him were all the unbeatable BMWs. Determined to get on terms with the BMWs, in 1960, Owen built a new, lower outfit, powered by a Triumph Tiger 100 engine, tipped as near horizontal as possible in an attempt to get the centre of gravity as low as the German flat-twin engines conducted by the likes of ace Max Deubel.

Achieving ninth place in the 1961 Sidecar TT, Owen was still occasionally racing solos. In 1963 he started his own tuning business, but had reached a plateau with his sidecar racing. The machine was handling well, but he was flogging the engine to death trying to stay with the BMWs, and rebuilds were expensive. Basically, nothing could match the 500cc RS54 Rennsport German engines, apart from, maybe, Chris Vincent's 'factory' 650cc BSA,** occasionally. Owen couldn't afford a BMW machine at £1200.

One has to sympathise with the frustrated Owen's predicament. A talented racer on solos or sidecars, and a very practical mechanic who could design and construct, he nevertheless lacked the funds to compete against those using superior machines. All the elements were in place for a perfect storm in the sidecar racing world.

It all came down to engine power. With the advent of the 1275cc Mini Cooper 'S,' the earlier 1071cc 'S' units were becoming available secondhand. However, this unit didn't lend itself to being fitted in a motorcycle frame, so why not use a Mini front end complete, with a wheel at the back? Morgan three-wheelers had raced sidecars over the years, but even the postwar trend to put two 500cc Speedway JAP barrels on a new crankcase wasn't enough for Owen. Even Mogvin, the Vincent rear end with Morgan suspension front-end, didn't appeal.

Owen regarded all of the power going through a single back wheel as an Achilles heel. ACU (Auto Cycle Union) regulations didn't rule out a symmetrical three-wheeler, as opposed to the sidecar's asymmetry, also, and here's where it gets controversial. If wheel centres were less than 8in (203mm) apart they counted as one wheel! Sensing potential aggravation from the scrutineers, Owen ensured the distance was below the limit. No doubt he read and re-read the crucial paperwork before he committed a penny or cut steel, and concluded that his brainchild was viable.

So, starting off with a Mini front end, and the help of a BRM chassis designer and Rolls-Royce panel worker, the soon-to-be notorious Owen Greenwood Mini was completed in March 1965, after three months' work. Owen could not be accused of throwing money at it, using, as he did, mainly 'pre-owned' parts, and spending just £450.

MECHANIC OWEN GREENWOOD PORED THROUGH THE REGULATIONS IN ORDER TO CREATE HIS
CONTROVERSIAL – AND UNBEATABLE – GREENWOOD MINI. HE DROVE ROUND THE OUTSIDE
OF SIDECARS ON BENDS. THE CAR COULD BITE BACK IF PROVOKED.

13

REGULATIONS STATED THAT IF TWO WHEELS
WERE WITHIN A CERTAIN DISTANCE OF EACH
OTHER THEY COUNTED AS ONE!

G.H 13

To Boldly Go

Mechanicals and 'body'

The original Mini has a self-contained power unit, and suspension that sits in a subframe. The only separate element is the steering-rack, which is usually bolted to the bodyshell toe-board. Using round and square steel tubing, a very simple semi 'bird-cage' chassis/body had a stressed aluminium skin riveted to it.

The rear-end used two Mini trailing arms, inverted and facing inward, with non-standard coilover damper units; front suspension was Alex Moulton's standard rubber 'blocks.' The wheelbase was 6in (152mm) shorter than a Mini's. Rear wheels were standard Mini Cooper; fronts were 6.5in (165mm) alloys with Cooper disc brakes.

The Cooper 'S' engine drank through a 45mm Weber twin-choke carburettor, and was cooled by a large, front-mounted radiator and oil cooler. A rare Colotti five-speed gearbox was used at one stage, (usually a close-ratio Mini Cooper box with a 3.76:1 final drive). 970cc, 1071cc and 1275cc engines were fitted, depending on circumstance. Eventual maximum power was a little over 90bhp at a shade over 8000rpm.

To allow the passenger to move around, a fuel tank was strapped outside the body adjacent to the driver, who, using normal car controls, sat low behind a power bulge covering the protruding carburettors, partially protected by a large fly-screen.

The vehicle weighed 5.7cwt (290kg), with over half of this being the compact but heavy Mini engine/gearbox/final drive. A Mini saloon weighed just over twice what the Greenwood Mini did.

During the initial 1965 campaign, a tendency for the unloaded inside wheel to waste power on bends by losing traction was cured by fitting a ZF limited-slip differential. Like all 'three-wheelers,' the suspension required an anti-roll bar to compensate for having only half the roll resistance of a normal four-wheeler.

Did the Greenwood Mini work?

It shows how good the BMW outfits were, because the Mini – timed at 118mph at Silverstone – wasn't as fast flat-out. Handling was safe, up to a point, as it tucked in under power and ran wide off throttle: this unconventional device's unique footprint meant that, 'in extremis,' all hell could break loose (which it did on a couple of occasions).

There was also a slight handicap, in that the impotently outraged ACU governing body decreed Owen must always start at the back of the grid! This wasn't just through spite. As the driver couldn't join in with the push-start like other outfits, a 'pusher' had to help the passenger. If near the front of a 30+ entry grid, a new 'pusher' would have been required for every race, due to the previous one getting the hedgehog treatment from an unsympathetic field.

With hindsight Owen felt his device could have been built lighter. Using the heavy Mini front subframe, although time-saving, could have been avoided, and a single rear wheel might even have been better. A racing sidecar outfit weighed about 200lb (90.5kg) less than the Greenwood Mini. The Mini Cooper gearchange wasn't as fast as a racing sidecar's sequential box.

Despite these reservations, in his first season Owen won the Gold Cup Sidecar meeting at Mallory Park, broke the lap record at Cadwell Park, and ended 1965 by winning the Brands Hatch shield for most successful 'sidecar' of the year. In the 1966 International at Brands Hatch, Owen beat all the best continental riders, including World Champion Fritz Scheidegger. *Motor* magazine in August 1966 reported the Greenwood Mini winning the *Daily Mail* Sidecar Race of the Year at Mallory Park, increasing the lap record from 83 to 85.56mph.

Campaigning in 1965, 1966 and 1967, Owen won over 100 races. In the second season's 37 races he was 3rd once, 2nd seven times, and 1st 29 times! Of course, he had to pass up to 36 outfits each time he won. The *Motor Cycle* in August 1966 stated that, at Silverstone Club circuit, the device bettered the sidecar lap record by three seconds, and was 0.43 seconds outside the car class record (NB: cars carried no passenger). Top speed was 109mph at this time, but the old 'What'll she do, mister?' has always been a secondary issue on race circuits, because maintaining speed through corners is usually the key. Best recorded speed was the FIM (Federation Internationale Motorcycliste) flying kilometre record, at 120.838mph.

Owen had correctly predicted that his symmetrical 'outfit' could turn left or right equally well, would be stable under braking, and, with two driven wheels, have good traction, the three areas that sidecars had problems with. *Motor Cycle*'s tester commented that, unlike many racing Mini saloons, the Greenwood Mini didn't smoke its tyres, had no wheelspin, and cornered better than Mini saloons – it concluded the Mini could get through Silverstone's Copse corner 10mph faster than a sidecar. Owen's 'loophole special' won the National Championships in 1966 and 1967.

Provocative, moi?

One can argue that Owen's endeavours, whilst perfectly legitimate, were basically unfair; 'Spirit of the Game' springs to mind. Nevertheless, the governing body, no doubt with gritted teeth, allowed his creation to compete. One can but imagine the reaction of fellow competitors. August 1966's *Motor*

magazine reported that the sidecar men were trying to ban Greenwood's 'baby.' Chris Vincent, a leading 'chairman,' tried to get a 750cc limit as early as 1965. The owner of Cadwell Park imposed his own limit of 970cc, the smallest 'S' engine. International racing wasn't possible, as, despite the vehicle being 'legal,' the ACU organising authority just couldn't swallow it, probably fearing a diplomatic row. Owen himself attended only UK National Status events; unless invited for spectator value, he avoided club meetings because "It was a bit like taking candy from a baby."

Although Owen never complained of any hostility from fellow racers, it's likely that the ongoing controversy, including press letters from some purists, became a little wearing. Deciding to focus on his business in Loughborough, he sold his provocative pet at the end of the 1967 season. It was campaigned with some success in 1968 and 1969, but an ACU handicapping system had by now caught up with it.

Conclusion

Although racing sidecar outfits were always evolving, they were essentially asymmetric three-wheelers based on a motorbike with an outrigged wheeled-platform on which a passenger could perch (hence 'a bit on the side').

Despite Owen's creativity and racing talent, he concluded that existing British motorcycle engines couldn't match the BMW flat-twins, and, necessity being the mother of invention, he was led to a solution so outrageous, effective, but – crucially – legal, that, despite baffling the authorities, they had to allow it, at least in the UK. Morgan three-wheelers had often raced against sidecars, but the Greenwood Mini added insult to injury by actually having four wheels! This unorthodox device dominated or at least badly rattled the fastest outfits, winning a large percentage of the races it entered, and holding a host of lap records. Demonstrated at a vintage meeting at Oulton Park in later years, it was obviously in a class of its own – particularly on corners.

Anyone giving a talk on vehicle design could mention Owen Greenwood's Mini as a brilliant example of lateral, out-of-the-box thinking. When you come up with a solution so far ahead of the opposition that the rules have to be re-written, you've achieved something truly memorable. Maybe the Greenwood Mini wasn't popular with the administrators, or some purists, but it certainly thrilled the race-going public, and remains a classic.

---

* Aerodynamics are key in racing. A designer's dream would be a shape-shifting car, morphing from a low aerodynamic drag shape for speed, to high-drag for braking or down-force for cornering. Despite short-lived attempts to allow minor adjustments to the front wing by driver or air pressure flexing the wing, it wasn't until 2011 that the Drag Reduction System (DRS) was written into the rules. This allowed the driver, under certain circumstances, to move a large flap in the rear aerofoil 'biplane' in order to increase speed and overtake. The 2010 controversy called 'Kneegate' was caused by McLaren and Ferrari drivers becoming adjustable aerodynamic devices themselves by guiding – by their hand or knee – air ducted though the cockpit onto the rear aerofoils. Steering with one hand at 200mph was frowned on, and, if coupled with the driver adjusting a knob or switch, resulted in no hands on the wheel.

** Chris Vincent's A65 BSA bettered the Mini in 1071cc guise at an early outing for it at Silverstone in 1965. A fired-up Chris also beat the BMW stars that day. But Greenwood soon got the hang of it.

Owen Greenwood's thoughts:
"Afterwards I went into the gents and heard Georg Auerbacher say. 'That bloody Mini goes well.'"

"I was waiting for the slide to stop when I saw the marshals running from their post. That really worried me; I thought 'ruddy 'ell, things must be bad!'"

"It didn't like going sideways, and that's a fact. When that happened you just had to let it go."

One of the quickest sidecar men remarked at Brands Hatch that a decent outfit would be faster round right-handers. "So I waited until we got to Paddock, a right hander, and passed him on the outside ..."

UNIPOWER GT
1966-1970

THE 'MINI MIURA' UNIPOWER GT CAPITALISED ON THE 1960S SEARCH FOR SOMETHING DIFFERENT TO THE MAINSTREAM. THIS MID-ENGINED POCKET SUPERCAR FROM PERIVALE WAS A SUPERIOR OFFERING.

GH 13

HOW LOW CAN YOU GO?

Launched at London's Olympia Racing Car Show, the low, sleek Unipower GT caused a stir, attracting the nickname of the 'Mini Miura.'

Apart from being an instant hit with the press and public, for this little fibreglass coupé to be compared to the Lamborghini was extraordinary. Both two-door fastbacks, one was powered by an exotic 3929cc transverse V12; the other by a humble 998cc transverse BMC Mini engine. The Miura dripped with international jet-set glamour, and was a product of the famous Italian factory of Sant'Agata Bolognese; the GT was the creation of a fork-lift truck manufacturer in North West London's Perivale.

Despite its humble origins, the Unipower bewitched its helpless admirers, many of whom lay siege over the years to Perivale's rare product, in the hope of eventually possessing one. The Japanese, always in tune with precious creations, collected as many as they could. As well as being a 'looker,' the little GT was dynamically potent enough to deliver the goods on road and track. This multi-faceted personality is worthy of study.

Background

The 1960s saw a lot of interest in individualism: pop music, pop art, pop fashion, a 'Do your own thing, man!' culture. Cars were omitted from this headlong rush for freedom of expression. Mainstream British sports cars, Jaguar E-Types, Austin-Healeys, Triumph TRs, MGBs, et al, were supplemented by the somewhat less hairy-chested MG Midgets/Sprites and Triumph

To Boldly Go

Spitfires. But these were establishment offerings, and not quite in keeping with the counter-culture 1960s; the ubiquitous Mini/Cooper was, however, as witnessed by the countless numbers of souped-up examples. Its giant-killer image – acquired from beating often embarrassingly bigger cars, including the MkII Jaguar and behemoth Ford Galaxy, on the track, and in rallying – complemented its anti-establishment appeal.

Against this backdrop, several enthusiasts/entrepreneurs realised the opportunity to use the mechanics of everybody's darling, the Mini, as the basis for a sporty, hopefully desirable, coupé (a case of history repeating itself, as the original Austin 7 also spawned a multitude of 'Specials'), amongst them Cox GTM, Deep Sanderson, Mini Marcos, Broadspeed Mini, Ogle SX1000 and Unipower GT. The Unipower GT was the cream of the crop, employing best race car practice of mid-engine layout, space frame chassis, wishbone suspension and the whole package wrapped in a slinky body.

Interesting creations have interesting people behind them. Ernie Unger had worked for Colin Chapman in early Lotus days, then joined Rootes Group as a development engineer involved with what became the Hillman Imp. Despite racing a Lotus for five years, no British sports car really grabbed his imagination. A small-car enthusiast, Unger was a fan of the little Fiat- and Simca-based coupés by Austrian engineer Carlo Abarth.

The 1959 BMC Mini threw a switch in Unger's brain, saying 'Lightweight GT.' By 1963 and now at Ford, his doodlings gelled. Through racing he teamed up with Val Dare-Bryan, who was involved in racing car design and manufacture. During 1964 a vehicle took shape with the help of a moonlighting Ford stylist, rumoured to have worked on the famous GT40. An 850cc development mule was thrashed around Brands Hatch, and an aluminium-bodied prototype built.

Again through a racing contact Unger got financial support and a place to build his dreamcar. Tim Powell manufactured fork-lift trucks and other specialised machinery at Universal Power Drives (UPD), Perivale. A small production line was established in a corner of the factory.

Mechanical ingredients

No one had explained to the Unipower's enthusiastic creators that all design is a compromise. With heroic indifference to the economies of part-bin carryover, virtually every major element of the car was non-standard, other than the engine – even the gearbox had options, including a unique final drive ratio. Key elements demonstrate why this little GT was so special:

- The Mini saloon engine is overhung, the weight being forward of the driveshafts. Keeping it facing the same way, but moving it to the back made the Unipower mid-engined.
- Engine was the 998cc Cooper with 55bhp at 5800rpm. The 1275cc Cooper S unit with 75bhp at 6000rpm was optional. Final drives were usually 3.44, but a 2.9 was available.
- The square-tube chassis appears scarily lightweight with no backbone, relying on triangulated front and rear side frames joined by skeletal, triangulated sills: the side frames are united by minimal cross-tubes. It appears to promise the torsional rigidity of a damp postcard, but clever triangulation works wonders, they say.
- Suspension is wishbones all-round with coilover damper units. Wheels carry a little negative camber, and the rears toe-in slightly to aid understeer – or combat oversteer.

- Unlike the Mini the steering rack is forward of the hubs, and is a left-hand drive Cooper S unit mounted upside down (where there's a will …).
- A gear change mechanism for rear-mounted Mini engines is awkward: the loads are high and everything is in the wrong place. In this case, the gearlever ended up on the right with a reversed gate, ie forward from 2nd to 1st, and from 3rd to 4th, the linkage at the rear is a creative collection of rods and cranks.
- The standard side-mounted radiator wasn't up to the job, and was replaced by one in the Unipower's nose.
- The new fuel tank was positioned at the base of the windscreen.

Body

- The obsession with getting any car with sporty pretensions as low as possible resulted in the Unipower's minuscule height of 40in (1016mm). This proximity to the ground, and the car's overall proportions, suited the 10in (254mm) wheels of the early Minis.
- The car's 64in (4166mm) overall length appeared longer because of the GT's lack of height. But the Unipower was indeed 45in (1143mm) longer than the Mini.
- Specialised Mouldings finessed the prototype's exterior, and took moulds for the fibreglass bodies. Unusually, the whole underside was covered. This go-ahead company also made Lotus Europa bodies and Harris Mann's BLMC's 1969 Zanda concept car.
- The style employed a Triumph Spitfire windscreen and metal surround; the rear screen was plastic.
- The entire rear body hinged backward

G.H.13

RUMOURED TO HAVE BEEN STYLED BY A FORD MOONLIGHTER WHO'D WORKED ON THE GT40, THE GT WAS SO LOW IT WAS HARD TO GET IN AND OUT OF, BUT THE PROPORTIONS SUITED THE 10in (254mm) MINI WHEELS.

'á la Miura,' and was secured by Triumph Spitfire/Herald bonnet lever-clips.

- Large air scoops were featured aft of the early Mini-style sliding windows.
- Lamps were off the shelf.
- Webasto style fabric sunroofs were offered.

Interior

Those determined enough to squeeze through the hatch-like doors and negotiate a way past the gearlever found themselves in a functional sports-machine interior. Two slim, black bucket seats with headrests enabled a comfortable reclining position. The thick leather-rim steering wheel, still a bit of a novelty, then felt just right: its three aluminium spokes looking good. The flat-sheet aluminium dashboard had a scattering of basic instruments and switches. This was a no-frills, no-nonsense, 'press-on' interior; just as well because the rear screen was prone to misting, and a bus could lurk in the rear three-quarter blind spot.

Weight + power + aerodynamics = performance

Losing the Mini's steel bodyshell, two subframes and a lot of glass should have made the Unipower lighter, and it did. However, the cars had the same compact but very heavy 3.2cwt (163kg) power unit. The Unipower brochure claimed a weight of 10cwt (508kg), whereas early Mini saloons were 11.5cwt (584kg). *Autocar* calculated that the UPD product was 9% lighter than the Mini.

The Unipower wheelbase was 4in (101mm) longer than the saloon's – the same as the Mini traveller/van. Having the weight nearer the ground helped handling, and distribution was 40/60 front/back. A mid-engined layout will also have better traction than front-wheel drive.

The A-Series engine was a veteran, even by the mid-1960s, but S engines, of various capacities – due to their track and rally success – were well-regarded as robust and tunable. Because anything that the engine achieved in the Mini could logically be bettered in the lighter car, what should interest us here is the additional difference the slippery body made.

Unusually for a low volume manufacturer, the Unipower GT benefited from wind tunnel development, though it's not really surprising when you consider the backgrounds of Ernie Unger and Val Dare-Bryan. The Unipower's initial coefficient of drag (Cd) was 0.37; the Mini's 0.46 – at speed, the Mini couldn't stay with the coupé. 1966 magazine road tests, however, comment on the fastback's vulnerability to side gusts, LJK Setright called it 'aerodynamic oversteer.'

Back in the Motor Industry Research Association (MIRA) wind tunnel, it's thought that the designers may have invented the air dam because that addition cured front end lift, which was the main problem. All later Unipowers had a chin dam and Cd of 0.32 (an experimental droop-snoop got it down to 0.29). With its small frontal area and smooth underbody (see McLaren F1), the car could pull higher gears than the saloon, and the 998cc achieved over 100mph: even an 850cc one-off topped the 'ton.' *Motor* magazine in 1968 timed the 1275 S-powered car at 110mph, and suggested there was still a bit to go.

How did the 'Mini Miura' fare in practice?

The Perivale package was delivered in January 1966 to much praise, including from the Godfather of small GTs, Carlo Abarth.

UPD was no back street or viaduct operation; perfection was the bottom

THE 1275cc MINI COOPER S ENGINE COMPLEMENTED THE PETITE COUPÉ'S APPEAL. A LITTLE EXTREME FOR ROAD USE, IT NEVERTHELESS PROVED EFFECTIVE ON THE TRACK.

line. The author visited the works in the late 1960s, where there was a neat production line and exemplary standards.

The first year of production was slow because of inevitable on-going development fixes and finessing details. With good reviews again at the 1967 Racing Car Show, orders were strong, and production was steady, if slow. Apart from the UK, cars went to America, Hong Kong, Switzerland, Portugal, and Italy (which caused a contretemps by trying to produce its own versions!).

The standard offering was the 998cc Cooper unit, with the 1275cc S optional; also a five-speed gearbox, different final drives and sunroof. Against the backdrop

of a factory geared up for heavy-duty products, the pretty little coupé looked like a delicate bloom in a vegetable patch. UPD had probably viewed the endeavour as an interesting sideline or hobby, and, after making 60 units, in late 1968 sold the project to Piers Weld-Forrester, a sometime racing driver and entrepreneur. Manufacturing moved to nearby Park Royal under the flag of UWF (Unger Weld-Forrester) trading as Unipower Cars.

A MkII version was shown at the 1969 Racing Car Show. Upgrades to make it a little more civilised included softer springs, Dunlop GT alloy wheels, face-level vents, rearranged instruments on a padded black fascia, black windscreen

To Boldly Go

surround, new rear lamps, and fine lines.

But the main thrust of UWF was competition, including a one-off carbon-fibre reinforced lightweight body by Specialised Mouldings, pioneer of the new wonder material. Unipowers had been raced from day one, but UWF got serious, qualifying 4th in practice at the 1969 Targa Florio. The carbon-fibre car was entered for Le Mans, setting a practice time of 5.15 (Renault Alpine 5.12), and recorded at 140mph on the Mulsanne Straight, using a 1340cc works engine. Despite this promise, it failed to qualify.

Regardless of full order books, racing had drained production effort, and UWF ceased trading in January 1970, after contributing 15 units to the Unipower GT's total of 75.

Summary and conclusion

Road test interpretation requires the usual reading between the lines. The Unipower GT being so obviously created *by* enthusiasts *for* enthusiasts, and even connoisseurs, meant that magazines were refreshingly honest about it. It looked as if it meant business – sleek and low with big rear air scoops, and just generally desirable.

However, it was, in many ways, an impractical road car: hard to get in and out of, even Minis towered above it, and don't mention lorries, rear three-quarter blind spots, noise, prone to side-gusts, and an occasionally resentful gear change. But – and it's a big but – it was fun and fast, and afforded good handling.

John Baggott's book, *Mini: The Racing Story*, describes the Unipower's extensive motorsport life, including international, club, and historic events. People don't race vehicles unless they feel they are in with a chance. Many were subsequently converted to wide, 13in (330mm) wheels, flared eyebrows, and huge front air dams to maximise this potential. Slung low in a Unipower, you always knew that this was a racer rather than Grand Tourer.

Several eventually went to Japan, and the remainder are beyond any rational financial valuation. Considering its appealing blend of engineering and art, it was a bit of a mystery why no stylist stepped forward to take a bow for their contribution, although recently Unger identified Ford's Don Bradshaw as such.

Desirable, but expensive to build, the Unipower GT succumbed to the bane of small production economics: profitability. Ultimately, there was only so much you could charge for a Mini-powered car, however sophisticated and appealing. A Mini Cooper S in 1964 cost about £700, whereas early 998cc Unipowers were nudging £1000, and in 1967 1275cc S versions were approaching £1200.

This devotee's last sighting was in the 1970s, as an acid green example cruised past London's Royal Albert Hall. The 'Mini Miura' was a class act: a lump of cast iron, steel tubing and fibreglass fashioned into a jewel.

Some say that this was the best thing that ever happened to an A-Series engine.

An enthusiastic, but frustrated, LJK Setright in October 1967's *CAR* magazine complained: "The idea of exploiting this ready-made power egg seems analogous to dancing a foxtrot in Wellington boots."

Required to keep 10in (254mm) wheels for some race regulations, one Gerry Hulford eagerly exploited the famous Tyrrell P34 six-wheeler front tyres, which proved ideal for the Unipower.

BRITISH LEYLAND MOTOR CARS – ZANDA DESIGN STUDY

1969

BLMC'S 1969 ZANDA PROVED THAT THE UK COULD MATCH AND EVEN BETTER ANYONE AT STYLING 'CONCEPT CARS.' HARRIS MANN'S TOUR DE FORCE SET NEW STANDARDS FOR STYLING MOCK-UPS.

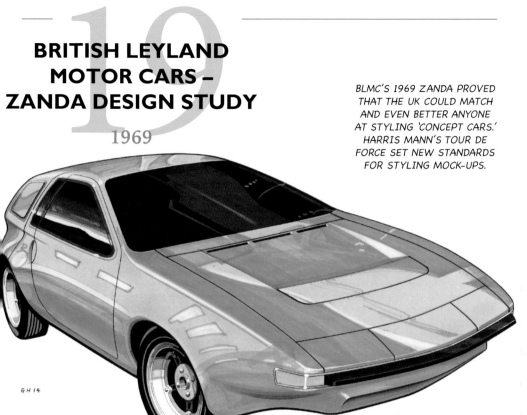

GH 14

AND THEN WE WERE FAB

Breakthroughs of any kind tend to be rare, and are often only recognised with hindsight. The British motor industry produced two scorching design exercises in 1969 and 1970, which deserve a place in any motoring hall of fame: British Leyland Motor Cars' (BLMC) Zanda, and Vauxhall's Styling Research Vehicle (SRV), covered in Chapter 21.

Background

The 1960s trigger for cultural change focused on lifestyle, with music supplying the back-beat as an understandable reaction to the somewhat low-key 1950s. The design world in general was also at the centre of the revolution, but the car industry was a bystander by comparison. Pop stars and the like were cheerfully 'souping-up' Minis, and even painting Rolls-Royce motor cars in psychedelic colours, but the production presses were still stamping out a previous generation's motoring solutions.

The energy of the 1960s erupted like a volcano, but appeared to have little effect on car design. The changing mood of the time was mainly reflected in low-volume sports cars, driven more by racing evolution than the Beatles. Of course, culturally, the '60s hardly began until around 1963. The mainstream motor men, even if they had been 'turned-on,' would have struggled to produce 'swinging' motor cars in that decade, due to production lead times of at least four years. Mass-produced car aesthetics were largely treading water, more focused on issues such as the elimination of lead-loaded body joints than 'flower power.' Also, the tidal wave of new legislation threatened to overwhelm even the mightiest resources.

Sociology students might well reflect on the dichotomy between the 'children of the revolution' with their long-haired 'love-ins,' etc, challenging traditional concepts of discipline and authority, and a car industry that was having the straps on its straightjacket tightened by ever stricter constraints by the legislature.

During the run-up to the 1970s, the mass-produced car choice was between Sir Alec Issigonis' brilliantly packaged two-box bodies, scaled-down Americana, or, at best, in BL's case, the Italian school. Pininfarina, after the excellent Austin A40 (1958-67), tried to influence BL towards the modernity and aerodynamic design that was finally employed in Citroën's GS (1970).

Manufacturing inertia in the UK was compounded by a general lack of commitment, or, indeed, awareness of the design discipline. Car aesthetics went under the title of 'styling,' which implied cosmetically draping a hopefully acceptable shape over an established engineering package. However, just as British art colleges had fuelled a lot of 1960s counter-culture, pop music and fashion, by the end of the decade they had turned their attention to the car world. The Royal College of Art (RCA) set up an Automotive Design course, to combine art and engineering. This initiative, along with other colleges, would eventually have an impact, but not for some years.

Revelation

Considering the industry's moribund

and hardly 'with-it' background, what appeared on the Earls Court Motor Show stand in 1969 was a minor miracle. Against the run of play, the Austin Morris Design team at Longbridge, under ex-Ford man Roy Haynes, showed a concept car called Zanda, conceived by Harris Mann.

Shyly displayed on the discreet stand of BLMC's body supplier, Press Steel Fisher (PSF), was a perfectly proportioned, practical, two-seater, mid-

LEADING DIRECTLY TO HARRIS MANN'S AUSTIN ALLEGRO, AUSTIN PRINCESS AND TRIUMPH TR7, SOME SAY ZANDA IS EVIDENCE OF AESTHETICS-DRIVEN DESIGN UNFETTERED BY PRODUCTION ENGINEERING DOMINANCE.

G.H 14

engine coupé, with fresh aesthetics from nose to tail. As a student on the RCA course I was simply amazed. This was no overblown 'Dream Car' indulgence, the usual flight of fancy, but an exciting glimpse of the obtainable future.

Essentially a sharp-nosed aerodynamic wedge with raked windscreen and chopped tail, it had a perfect, squat stance, sitting on its bolted-rim alloy wheels shod with the then novel low-profile tyres.

The pent-up energy of a new era had finally blown a hole through the crust of the established motor industry. To appreciate why Zanda was so potent in 1969, one only has to consider the contemporary BLMC offerings. The Mini Clubman, with its squared-up front and wind-up windows, had just been launched alongside predictable Fords and Vauxhalls – nothing approached Zanda's panache and brio. Apart from the bold wedge theme, what was

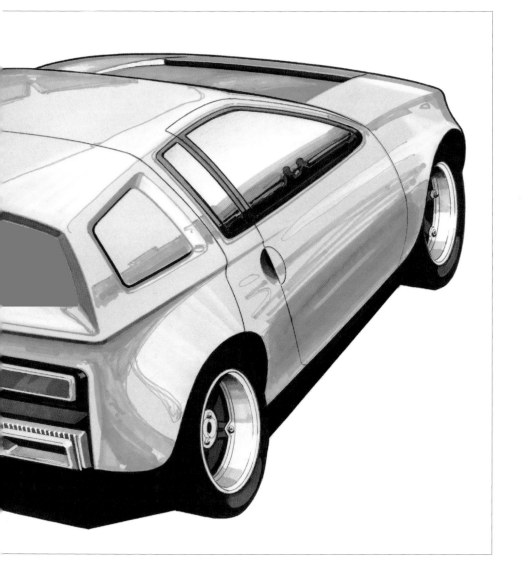

shockingly striking about Harris Mann's tour de force was the way he removed visual mass from under the vehicle corners via wheel cut-outs. This novel ploy encouraged the eye to linger on the wheels, which appeared proud of the body, but visually supported by the sculptured and flared wings. This gave the compact vehicle a presence, and a sense of being well-planted.

At this time many cars were styled from front, side and rear elevations, which were simply joined together at the corners. After admiring the featured wheels, Zanda's sculpturally relieved lower corners caused the eye to slip round the car: a good example of design in the round. The rear quarter-panel was saved from a 'Ferrari Breadvan' jibe by a clever floating panel that scooped cooling air in at the front, and allowed hot air to be sucked out from the trailing edge. Door side-glass was fixed, with an opening glass ventilation panel adjacent, which also helped over-the-shoulder vision.

The back window was heavily recessed, beneath which a graphically strong black panel led down to an eye-catching cast exhaust box.

Such was the vehicle's overall visual impact that the large rectangular exhaust outlets and featured circular door handle recesses could almost be taken for granted. The one-piece, cut-into-roof doors, now common, provided very rigid door sealing at motorway speeds. How engineers would have loved this last feature, but not the hinging of the rear bodywork, as on the 1972 Lancia Stratos. Concealing the windscreen wipers under a flap would guarantee a high level 'debate' (shouting match), as outraged feasibility engineers reminded the styling/designers about ice, or the flap closing mid-wipe cycle.

Not only was the adventurous shape right, but so, too, was the vehicle's technical package. It was engineered around an Austin Maxi's 1500cc engine and transmission, transferred wholesale to the rear in a similar way to the 1972 Fiat X1/9. Zanda featured a front-mounted radiator, its cooling air gulped by a large, under-nose mouth, with outlet vent on the bonnet top.

The project majored on the new Computer Aided Design (CAD) tooling facility, which PSF wanted to promote, but the styling process remained traditional pen and paper, with a clay mock-up leading to a fibreglass replica.

That Zanda appeared rather modestly under the PSF flag eloquently demonstrates BLMC's attitude to styling design. However, the design world 'got it' straight away, and it's certainly true that BLMC management woke up to Harris' talent.

Regardless of personal taste, one has only to look at the worthy but leaden 1964 1800 'Land Crab,' and the step-change resulting in the 1975 Austin Princess, to realise that a page had been turned. The Princess' low, long nose, raked screen, overall wedge and relatively short tail all reflect Zanda DNA. The Triumph TR7's 'blade' nose and pop-up headlamps are also the same kith and kin.

Summary

It is salutary to remember that when Zanda broke cover, the Morris Marina was still two years away, and the MGF over a quarter of a century! The Austin Maxi, Issigonis' final offering, was launched earlier in 1969. Appearing on the BBC, BLMC's American Director of Marketing described it, straight-faced, as having 'aggressive styling.'

Thankfully, the Zanda full-size model has survived, and can be seen at the Gaydon Heritage Centre, so you may view it in wonder, set amongst its contemporaries.

Harris Mann then had to cope with the mighty workload of the Allegro, TR7, Princess, and others. Harris, who I've since had the pleasure of working with, is a true enthusiast. Possibly, the Fiat 850 Coupé he was running at the time influenced his thinking somewhat, especially Zanda's admirably compact dimensions of length 142in (3600mm), width 61in (1550mm), and height 43in (1100mm).

Apart from being extraordinarily forward-thinking, Zanda helped set a trend for showing fibreglass replicas taken from clays. Now normal practice, these replicas allow a chance for debate before committing hundreds of millions to tooling, or new factories. Significantly, the replica work was done by Specialised Mouldings of Huntingdon, which also made bodies for the Lotus Europa and Unipower GT, both the epitome of 1960s cool.

No disrespect intended, but the funny thing about Zanda was the direction from which it came. The only people who really believed in the importance of styling/design were the Americans, who had been majoring in the subject for years, and had fabulous facilities. Against the odds, Harris Mann, like a magician, had pulled a very attractive rabbit out of the less-than-fashionable Longbridge hat.

> **Harris Mann on Sir Alec Issigonis:**
> "He had a big influence on me. But Issigonis wouldn't talk to me because I didn't have an engineering degree."

BOND BUG

1970-1974

OGLE DESIGN CHIEF TOM KAREN PROVED THAT MIGHTY SPECIFICATIONS AND RESOURCES ARE NOT ESSENTIAL IN CAR DESIGN. FROM EVERY ANGLE, THE ORANGE WEDGE GRABS ATTENTION; PARTICULARLY ITS UNABASHED REAR ASPECT.

GH 14

ANY COLOUR YOU LIKE AS LONG AS IT'S ORANGE

E
ven those willing to give three-wheelers the benefit of a very big doubt usually grimace at the single wheel at the front layout. Imagine the surprise, then, in 1970, when Bond revealed to an unsuspecting world the overtly sporty, orange, wedged, wrong-way-round trike that was the Bug.

Background

1970 was still at the epicentre of the 'anything goes' counter-culture of the swinging '60s. Mainstream manufacturers were struggling to keep up with a new youth market which, although enthusiastic for change, often didn't have a lot of money. Spotting an opportunity, the trio of Reliant, Bond and Ogle Design

united to create a unique, attractive, reasonably priced and practical offering, projecting a cool 'with-it' attitude.

Due to the use of a simple chassis and the low tooling costs of a fibreglass body, this trio could move quickly enough to match the mood of the time. Reliant had recently bought out Bond, its only competitor. Bond had tried to take on Tamworth's commercially successful vehicles with its 875, its Hillman Imp rear end directed by a single front wheel.

Coincidentally, the 007 association of 'Bond' probably didn't do any harm at all.

Mechanicals

The Bug used a clever adaptation of Reliant's simple, robust, and yet to be announced 1973 Robin chassis and mechanics. Sensibly, the weight of occupants, engine, fuel tank and battery

116

was pushed as far rearward as possible, toward the stable end of the triangle – the live rear axle. It was essentially mid-engined, the all-alloy unit living inside the cabin under a large, removable hump. Tricycle tax stipulated a weight of under 8cwt (406.4kg), and the resultant 7.8cwt (395kg) was made possible by clever details like moulded-in seats, plastic side screens, and small rear window glass.

Introduced with 700cc, then upgraded to 750cc, many surviving examples use the later Reliant Robin 850cc unit (41bhp). This is a useful overhead valve engine, which the 750 Motor Club extensively used in its popular racing formula. Terminal velocity was something under 80mph, and, perhaps due to respectable aerodynamics, compared favourably to a 850cc Mini or 875cc Hillman Imp.

Tellingly, the Bug also cost a bit more than these two 'proper' cars. Unusually, *Autocar* and *Motor* magazines of June 1970 both gave the three-wheeler full tests and write-ups. As well as the Mini and Imp they published figures from a Honda N600G, Fiat 500L, Fiat 850, Triumph 650 sidecar unit, NSU Super Prinz, and Steyr-Puch 650TR11. Obviously, both magazines took the new arrival seriously enough to grant it honorary four-wheeler status, because of their readers' interest in this novel newcomer.

The Bug was amongst the last generation of motor vehicles that a home mechanic could reasonably get to grips with, so anyone familiar with models such as the 1930s Austin 7 would not be fazed.

Body

The key styling ploy was to exploit the then fashionable wedge shape, the fibreglass body neatly wrapping round this little pod. It was cleverly made out of just two main mouldings: the body and the roof. Cute frog-eye headlamps also helped aesthetic appeal. The abruptly chopped off rear, accommodating a weekend bag and spare wheel, was the perfect packaging and aerodynamic solution.

One might question the lack of a deep front apron to discourage air from lifting the nose at speed, but no road test found it aerodynamically unstable; the sloping bonnet and windscreen doubtless keeping the front pressed down. All in all, it's hard to conceive of a better way of dressing this – albeit unconventional – package.

Daringly, the style flaunted an exposed rear axle and visible coil springs, this novel ploy effectively cocking a snook at the hitherto perceived inherent instability of such a trike. And anyway, 'letting it all hang out' was very much in vogue, lifestyle-wise (witness the Beach Buggy), and was all grist for the image mill.

This rear suspension arrangement was indeed quite sophisticated, with coilover dampers, four trailing arms, Panhard rod and anti-roll bar. The Bug's inward-sloping body sides emphasised the vehicle's relatively wide rear aspect of 55in (1397mm) and chunky alloy wheels: it didn't look as if it would easily fall over. The 10in (254mm) Dunlop alloy wheels seem small today, but this is what the original 'right-on' Mini wore, and they saved weight.

Even the Bug's saucily exposed rear suspension was upstaged when, to allow access, the entire cabin front, including windscreen and side-screens, was swung up and forward on a damped strut. This piece of theatre conjured up genuine Lamborghini-style drama.

The Bug's side-screens, which were, of course, removable, did offer an escape route if this orange wedge found itself inverted and resting on its roof for any reason.

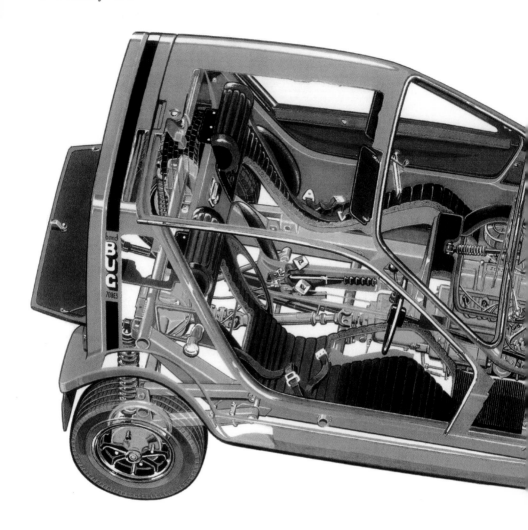

Really interesting designs can usually be traced back to one prime mover, and in this case our hero was Tom Karen, a very experienced car styling designer. Starting at Ford, he went on to be top man at Ogle Design consultancy, and arguably, with the 1968 Reliant Scimitar GTE, the originator of the sports estate. A sometime tutor at the Royal College of Art's (RCA) Automotive Design course, Karen influenced the likes of Peter (McLaren F1) Stevens, and, if I may modestly say so, your author.

On the road

Driving past the UK's Motor Industry Research Association (MIRA) on Watling Street, the old Roman road, in early 1970, this extraordinary, still secret orange wedge emerged, then disappeared in the opposite direction. Dangerously distracted by watching it in the rear view mirror, I noted its fifth (fourth), data-logging wheel trailing behind, signifying a road test car.

This was a first pre-launch sighting of what soon became known as the Bond

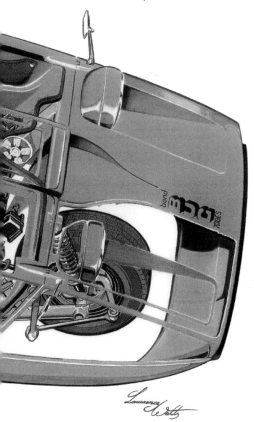

in truth, very little. It was fresh, fun and 'far-out man,' to quote the idiom of the day.

Tom bravely invited a small group of RCA students, including this scribe, to drive the pre-production Bug around Ogle's Letchworth Garden City. With valve bounce in every gear and anti-roll bar straining on roundabouts, it was harmless and innocent fun, and grabbed a lot of attention. Stopping to change drivers in the High Street, and lifting that great orange canopy was not recommended for shrinking violets, because everybody wanted to have a look. The exposed, low-slung seats, black doughnut steering wheel, stubby gearlever, and 1930s radiogram speedo didn't disappoint.

Of course, to catch-out this trike's layout at any speed all you had to do was wrench the steering wheel and hit the brakes. With all the weight thrown to the unsupported corner, you'd lift a wheel and possibly ignominiously tip the device on to its side, or actually roll it. Apparently, a journalist did just that at the press launch; likewise Jeremy Clarkson on BBC's *Top Gear* during his not-so-clever demolition of Reliant Robins, years later.

Driven within its limits, the Bug felt nippy and stable. Being relatively light, acceleration felt at least as lively as that of the 850cc Mini or 875cc Hillman Imp, although, of course, there was no contest when it came to cornering. It seemed a bit of a time-warp between a super modern style, covering what even then felt rather old-fashioned engineering. But it worked, was enjoyable, and will always remain so.

What happened next

This idiosyncratic, unconventional niche product from a niche manufacturer fascinated national newspapers and

Bug. Students at the RCA occasionally saw Tom Karen if he was in London. I remember saying to him that the orange wedge was sensational and exciting, even considering Kensington's Lamborghini Miuras that we were used to seeing (this was possibly a little sycophantic, looking back). My comments made his day, as we were the target age group customer.

Its easy to dismiss the Bug now as a one-minute-wonder, but Tom Karen at Ogle should be lauded for making something out of, if not nothing, then,

To Boldly Go

motoring journals alike, the cheeky little wedge attracting great publicity. The *London Evening Standard* called it a 'Chelsea boot on wheels,' after the stylish popular footwear, and mused at length over whether this was the car for the seventies.

Often photographed in trendy Carnaby Street, the Bug's star initially burned very brightly. On sale from June 1970 to May 1974, 2268 examples were made. Perhaps the reality of its limitations eventually dampened its appeal, but it remains instantly recognisable today, and very collectable.

Reliant built a four-wheeled prototype, and post-Reliant Bugs were produced, including a four-wheeler, but, truth be told, affordable mainstream cars were now just too good for the Bug to be anything other than an interesting cultural sideshow.

Tom Karen's success was in his ability to create an instantly recognisable, often referenced, vehicle. You may like the Bug (and I do), or laugh at it (and I don't), but it is a textbook example of a designer's prime role: that of visual communicator.

To exhibit at the four-wheeler-only Earls Court Motor Show, a back-to-back Bug was built – a long, orange, push-me-pull-you.

After the Bug's launch, trying to appear sophisticated, I asked Tom Karen if it was a 'loss leader' for the next Reliant family three-wheeler, I left the stage to the sound of my own footsteps: lead and balloon come to mind …

As the ferry pulled away heading for the Isle of Wight in 1970 – a family holiday accidentally coinciding with the notorious pop festival – I looked at a brand new Bug parked on the quay, definitely a counter-culture moment for this simple machine, the motoring equivalent of Andy Warhol's '15 minutes of fame.'

VAUXHALL STYLING RESEARCH VEHICLE (SRV)

1970

VAUXHALL'S 1970 SRV. THE HATCH REAR DOOR AND LACK OF A B/C POST BETWEEN THE DOORS IS AN INCREASINGLY ATTRACTIVE CONCEPT TO DESIGNERS. BLMC'S ZANDA (IN GREEN) PUT VAUXHALL TO THE TEST.

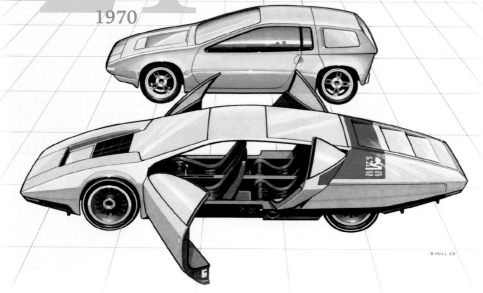

G.HULL 03

LUTON'S FINEST FLIGHT OF FANCY

The original believers in the importance of styling/design were the guys who invented marketing, the Americans, and they always had no-expense-spared facilities. In the industry, GM was generally considered top gun; certainly its artwork, to any impressionable young student, appeared to be in a class of its own.

Background – Luton's styling temple

GM's premier outpost in Europe, and certainly in the UK car industry, was Vauxhall's Luton studios. GM also organised its unique Craftsman's Guild Competition for would-be stylists to create a model futuristic car. Many wide-eyed visitors to the Luton facilities, after

Vauxhall and Styling Design moved out in the 1980s, found it hard to believe that this secret temple to the goddess of automotive aesthetics existed in a fairly mundane monolithic office block. It was a superbly equipped engineering centre, its pièce de résistance a vast rooftop viewing area with several studios opening on to it. In the late 1960s, it must have seemed like car styling heaven to those lucky enough to work there.

Supremacy challenged – and answered

When the cosseted inhabitants of this Luton dream factory saw the British Leyland Motor Cars (BLMC) Zanda concept car in 1969, they must have been stunned, because, a year later at the Earls Court Motor Show, Vauxhall's Assistant Design Director, Wayne Cherry, an American from Indianapolis, wheeled out

THE SRV IS THE MOST EXTREME COMBINATION OF AESTHETIC AND ENGINEERING DESIGN TO EMERGE FROM THE UK AUTO INDUSTRY. IT IS WIDER THAN A ROLLS-ROYCE AND ALMOST AS LONG, YET LOWER, THAN A MINI.

their response. Not withstanding Detroit's history of one-off exercises, the Vauxhall Styling Research Vehicle (SRV) was really something else, and perhaps never bettered as a showpiece of automotive design enthusiasm and ability.

Published sequential renderings by Chris Field, SRV's exterior designer, clearly show a Zanda-like profile as a starting point, the shape morphing into a much longer, more extreme, four-seat aerodyne. On the 1970 Motor Show stand, in all its well-lit silver glory, it was a sensational sight, only 3.5in (89mm) shorter than a Rolls-Royce Silver Shadow, 4.25in (111mm) wider, and almost 12in (296mm) lower than a British Leyland Mini.

Longer, lower and wider are the trinity that styling designers ache for, even if usually only adjusting an existing design by millimetres (see VW Golf

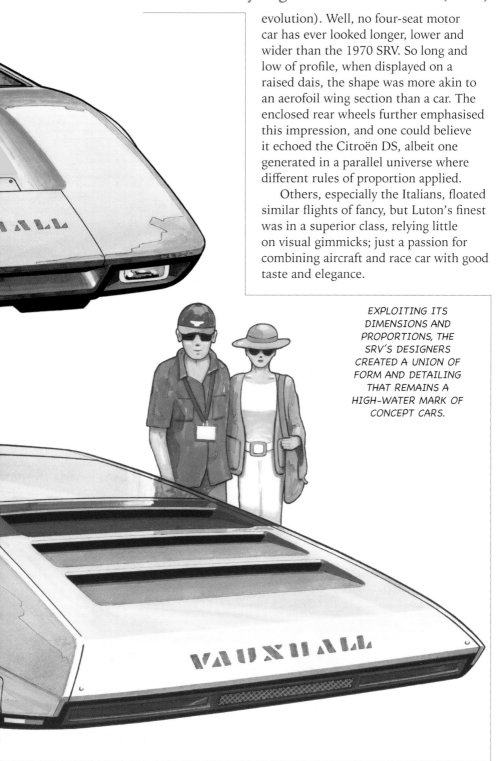

evolution). Well, no four-seat motor car has ever looked longer, lower and wider than the 1970 SRV. So long and low of profile, when displayed on a raised dais, the shape was more akin to an aerofoil wing section than a car. The enclosed rear wheels further emphasised this impression, and one could believe it echoed the Citroën DS, albeit one generated in a parallel universe where different rules of proportion applied.

Others, especially the Italians, floated similar flights of fancy, but Luton's finest was in a superior class, relying little on visual gimmicks; just a passion for combining aircraft and race car with good taste and elegance.

EXPLOITING ITS DIMENSIONS AND PROPORTIONS, THE SRV'S DESIGNERS CREATED A UNION OF FORM AND DETAILING THAT REMAINS A HIGH-WATER MARK OF CONCEPT CARS.

To Boldly Go

The overall style defeats categorisation: is it a saloon car, a coupé, a sports car, or even a car at all? How does an origami-like shape of folded angles – reminiscent of a child's 'fold along the dotted lines' book – achieve such visual sophistication?

Further imagery is the obvious, usually gauche, ploy of using 'slimming' black paint on the lower surfaces. It becomes apparent that a shape that grabs the attention so powerfully is just a side elevation joining front and rear elevations, all of which, it seems, could have been carved out of wood. Oh dear, does our paragon of aesthetic endeavour have feet of clay?

Why does this SRV look so good?

So what is the secret, the alchemy that transforms the average into styling gold? It's all about proportion, and further emphasising an already long, wide and low shape. SRV's 105in (2670mm) wheelbase has unusually long front and rear overhangs, highlighting the vehicle's length. Its width allows extreme tumble-home (ie angle of side-glass); in turn, packaging the occupants, shoulder-to-shoulder. In fact, occupants are so far inboard that most of the sill section has to come away with the door to allow ingress and egress.

Because of the length, the roof can fall in an unbroken line from the low windscreen header to the low tail. In styling parlance, the basic shape is a 'form study,' which then carries graphic elements: witness the perfect side-glass shape; the raked windscreen feeding down into a modular, black panel of motorised hinged flaps (concealing headlamps and wipers).

The red, rear quarter graphic featuring the Vauxhall Griffin and Union Jack is well considered, and helps to conceal the rear 'hatch' doors – such a bold,

audacious counterpoint has probably only ever been echoed by the Audi R8's contrasting side panel.

The louvres covering the rear window are as well executed as anything seen anywhere. The rear lamps, usually made the most of in order to break up heavy rear ends, are semi-concealed in SRV's elegantly slim tail.

The fundamental, unique nature of this vehicle's architecture, coupled with cunning artifice and surface tension, creates a form the like of which has not been seen before ... or since.

Technicals

SRV's technical specification still excites. It had a mid-mounted, transverse, turbocharged engine – turbos were not common streetware at this time; the chassis and body used aluminium honeycomb and carbon fibre; self-levelling rear suspension, with an adjustable front wing to trim out the vehicle attitude in motion; a data collection system, including pitot tube sensors, to aid aerodynamic fine tuning, along with subtly incorporated aircraft type airflow guide fins.

It had fixed seats with adjustable squabs and controls, and fuel tanks, including under-the-front seats, with a fuel transfer pumping system for ideal weight distribution. In all, the technology of an earth-bound aircraft with race car underpinnings.

Interior

The rear-hinged supplementary rear 'hatch' doors, and associated deletion of a BC pillar, allowed dramatic appreciation of the interior, and as ease of ingress/egress, this feature becoming increasingly popular some 40 years later. The interior was a lesson in simplicity, and the opposite of today's – some argue – excessively feature-rich approach.

Radically, there was no instrument panel or dashboard – instruments and supplementary controls were either in the doors, or on a hinged-module that swung out with the driver's door.

SRV's heritage

While BLMC's 1969 Zanda was only a see-through fibreglass shell, the Vauxhall had opening doors, boot and bonnet, and a real interior, all carried on a rolling chassis complete with mocked-up engine. The device still exists, and is occasionally dusted down for enthusiasts to appreciate at special events.

Over the years, this admirer has met several of the people who worked at Luton during this project, from the workshop technician who made the front aerofoil to Wayne Cherry. Wayne mentioned owning a gunmetal Rolls-Royce Silver Cloud convertible with a red interior. John Stephenson, who went on to be Director of Product Planning at Rolls-Royce, Crewe, designed some clever door hinges, and other working details. John Heffernan and Ken Greenley, known for their work on the Panther Solo and Bentley Continental R, were also in the studios at this time, as was Geoff Lawson who became Design Director at Jaguar. All those involved, either directly or by the association of simply being there, remember the project with affection and pride.

Anyone wishing to recharge their creativity batteries could do a lot worse than track down issue 28 of the Italian publication *Style Auto Architettura della Carrozzeria,* and get a neat hit of SRV. Chris Field's exterior renderings and John Taylor's under-the-skin drawings are as near to undiluted enthusiasm as one is ever likely to see. The project also gives

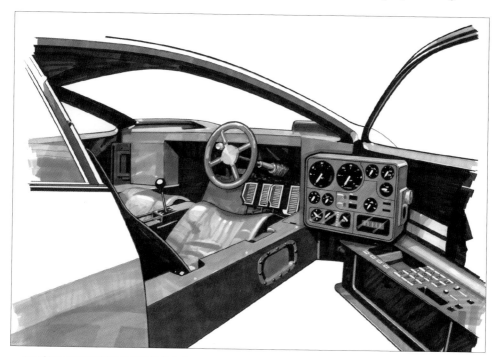

DESPITE THE EXTREME NATURE OF THE EXTERIOR, THE SRV'S RESTRAINED INTERIOR IS THE OPPOSITE OF THIS CENTURY'S FEATURE-RICH APPROACH. THERE IS NO FASCIA: A HINGED MODULE AND DOORS CARRY READ-OUTS AND CONTROLS.

To Boldly Go

a lie to the old accusation that 'styling' is just cosmetic, because all of the vehicle packaging and detail was resolved within the 'styling design' discipline. There is no doubting Chris Field's talent as he won the Institute of British Carriage and Automobile Manufacturers (IBCAM) and *Daily Telegraph* competition in 1972, with his Aquila, based on the Austin Maxi. A runner was built under the supervision of George Moseley, Chief Designer at Mulliner Park Ward.

Conclusion

Admittedly only conjecture, but it does appear that the superlative Vauxhall Styling Design centre was stung into action by Harris Mann's Zanda concept study. Surrounded by bread-and-butter production offerings such as the Viva, Firenza, Chevette, Cresta, and Victor,

et al, a queasy list if ever there was one, Wayne Cherry and his team were possessed by a fine madness to show the world what they could really do. One could argue the SRV was pure theatre – totally impractical and irrelevant, with perhaps only the silver 'Droopsnoot' Firenza reflecting any of this nuclear burst of energy. But to this observer the SRV should be judged more as a work of art, a mobile sculpture, if you like. If such endeavours ever cease, humans will be the poorer for it.

It was only fitting that the UK, the country that contributed so much to the 1960s celebration of the love for life, should come up with first the BLMC Zanda, and then the Vauxhall SRV, both genuinely world class ground-breakers in their field.

Wayne Cherry:
"Designers always love to do two-seater sports cars because they're easy, but I don't think anyone had ever done a four-door coupé before."

John Stephenson:
"I was always very proud of the 'hidden' rear-hinged doors, because they eventually arrived in production on the [2001] Mazda RX-8." (Like the Mazda, the SRV had no pillar between the doors, which, when opened, displayed the entire uninterrupted interior.)
(Above quotes from *Classic & Sports Car*)

Indicative of the juxtaposition between this radical concept car and Vauxhall's usual fare, *Autocar* showed a cartoon of the SRV alongside the just-launched HC Viva, and captioned it "Any real connection?"

BRUBAKER BOX

1972-1979

THE BRUBAKER BOX WAS LIKE
NOTHING ON EARTH IN 1972. IT
PRE-EMPTED THE MULTI-PURPOSE
VEHICLE (MPV)/SPORTS UTILITY,
COMBINING A CONSPICUOUS
EXTERIOR WITH PARTIALLY
CONCEALED INTERIOR.

G.HULL 03

BOXING CLEVER

The laws governing the space/time continuum have fascinated writers from HG Wells through to Von Deniken. Some argue that Leonardo da Vinci was actually a marooned time-traveller. One hazard of time-travel is the danger of accidentally changing history: the risk being that such a traveller could drop, say, a sonic screwdriver in a previous century, and start a paradox chain of events resulting in their parents not meeting. Which means that the time-traveller would never have been born to drop the screwdriver. Complicated, isn't it ...?

Background

The Brubaker Box appeared out of the blue in the early 1970s on the American West Coast. As if slipping through a wormhole from a parallel universe or a time warp, it was obviously out of place in the normal scheme of things. One could imagine an ET-type life form, waiting for spare parts for their spaceship, amusing themselves by fashioning a runabout that reminded them of home.

Possibly Curtis Brubaker, the named designer, was an alien abductee, subconsciously influenced by an imperfectly wiped memory of something he'd seen while on the Mother Ship. The official story is that Brubaker saw California's Beach Boys using VW vans and Beach Buggies and fused the two together.

The impact of the design when it was unveiled in the States was understandably dramatic. The American magazine *Car and Driver* grabbed the prototype, and put it straight on to its March 1972 front cover, declaring all bets were off about the future of cars! The late 1960s was witness to the status quo in Detroit's America being badly shaken by imports. This sensational, VW-based device added insult to injury, as it was the result of fifth-columnist activity; being home-grown the vandals were inside the establishment walls.

From any angle, Brubaker's Box epitomised street cred that is still ahead of the game. Was it a car or a van? Crouching low and wide it looked tougher than most sports cars. The reaction to the prototype from the cool, normally unfazeable, Californians was wide-eyed, many assuming that it was powered by something edgy: a nuclear reactor, or a Wankel, at least. They sensed, instinctively, that the veil concealing the future had been lifted slightly. Lee Iacocca, Chrysler's biggest gun at the time, was apparently inspired to have a poster of the Box on his office wall.

Mechanicals

The advanced intelligence behind the Box was, of course, constrained by the simple materials to hand; thus underpinnings from a modified air-cooled VW Beetle platform had to suffice. This is a backbone chassis, with integral flat pressings each side forming the vehicle's floor. The front suspension's two transverse torsion-bars are bolted to the front, and two short trailing arms each side locate the hubs. The rear has similar torsion bars with trailing arms locating swinging axles. The final drive/gearbox/engine is cantilevered off the back of the chassis.

This platform is self-contained and separate from the body, so is easily shortened, and ideal for Beach Buggies.

The standard flat-four engines are

1285cc or 1493cc, producing 50 or 53bhp, but American tuners cheerfully went over 2000cc, so final power was a bit academic. Similarly, platform components can be extensively upgraded. Like Beach Buggies, the Box was a candidate for the extrovert chromed 'writhing snakes' exhaust systems.

The fuel tank was moved from the nose to the nearside, between the wheels. The pedals were moved forward and raised, and the steering column was shortened slightly.

Body

The extraordinary fibreglass body was 3.5in (89mm) lower than a Beetle, 1.5in (38mm) shorter, and 8.5in (216 mm) wider.

The one-box shape was emphasised by a black, grained roof that continued around the front and rear glass. The rear end stopped with an angled, recessed, backlight, a precursor to the later

THE WEST COAST SURFERS USED VW'S MICRO-BUSES/CAMPER VANS AND VANS, BUT ALONGSIDE THE BOX THE DIFFERENCE IS DRAMATIC.

G.HULL 04

sports/estate hatchback style. The lower front and rear ends were dramatically under-cut. The windscreen began right at the nose and was steeply raked back. Two enormous round headlamps dominated the front. The windscreen

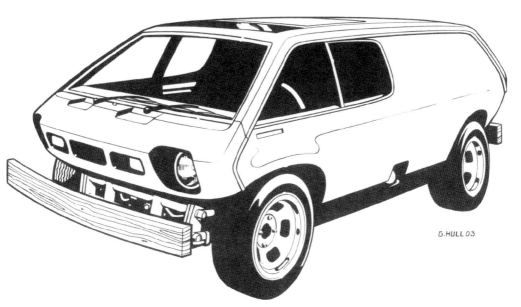

USING THE AIR-COOLED VW BEETLE PLATFORM, BRUBAKER EMPLOYED MECHANICAL ELEMENTS SUCH AS THE TWIN TORSION-BAR FRONT SUSPENSION. SLOT-STYLE ALLOY WHEELS DOMINATE.

G.HULL 03

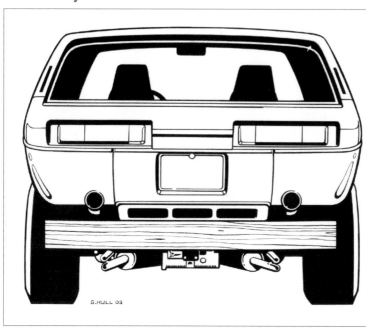

THE BRUBAKER BOX'S REAR VIEW WAS A FORERUNNER OF MANY NEXT CENTURY OFFERINGS. AGAIN, MECHANICAL ELEMENTS WERE ONLY PARTIALLY CONCEALED. ITS WIDE WHEEL STANCE SAID IT ALL. NOTE THE TIMBER-EFFECT, DAMPED, BUMPERS.

G.HULL 03

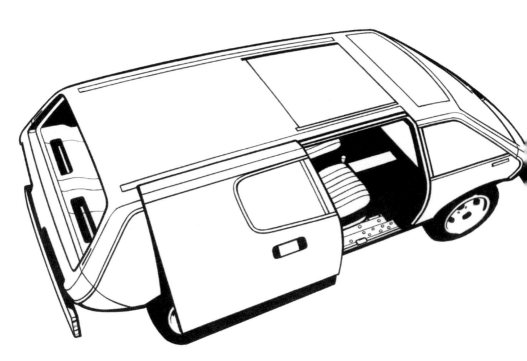

G.HULL 03

THE BOX HAD ONE DOOR, WHICH POPPED OUT, THEN SLID ALONG A CONCEALED ROOF TRACK.
A GLASS PANEL ABOVE THE WINDSCREEN AIDED THE DRIVER'S VIEW OF TRAFFIC LIGHTS. THE
ROOF LENT ITSELF TO CARRYING A LUGGAGE BOX, CAMPER TENT, BOAT, ETC.

and side glass seem to have been sourced from the Ford Pinto and AMC Gremlin; the Chevrolet El Camino supplied the backlight.

The Brubaker Box was asymmetrical, in that there was no roadside entrance, and everyone used the single entry on the kerbside. This door was an aircraft, or spaceship, type, which popped open then slid sideways – one had to smile when seeing the Peugeot 1007 concept at the 2004 Paris Motor Show demonstrating a similar door. As if the body's extreme nature wasn't already compelling enough, the vehicle sat on the biggest set of polished alloy wheels and fattest rubber then available. This was calculated to allow the wheels to dominate the style in a way that wouldn't be seen again until 30 years later, with BMW Minis on 17in rims.

Piston-mounted energy absorbing bumpers, finished in wood grain, protruded cheerfully into space.

Perhaps wood was a novelty on planet Thorg, or wherever 'Brubaker' really came from.

On an aesthetic level, the roof design was a masterstroke – the vinyl effect black top beautifully integrated additional glass above the windscreen, a sliding sunshine panel, and a track for the door. The designer envisaged a removable module on the roof to use as additional storage – or as a boat. A motorhome option was also considered with elevating roof and bunks, etc.

To improve field of vision, production versions had slightly longer side glasses. Discreet engine vents were introduced on the rear lower sides, and rear side-markers added,

If the radical shape didn't blow you away, the colour and finish would. A special, burnished-copper effect was featured on the sides and across the lower back panel. This unique metallic finish was polished and lacquered to

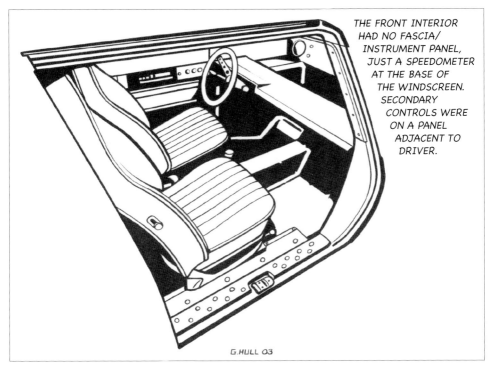

THE FRONT INTERIOR HAD NO FASCIA/INSTRUMENT PANEL, JUST A SPEEDOMETER AT THE BASE OF THE WINDSCREEN. SECONDARY CONTROLS WERE ON A PANEL ADJACENT TO DRIVER.

G.HULL 03

an extraordinary degree. The effect was similar to one of those seductive limpid 'walls' that science fiction characters disappear through into another dimension (no surprise there).

Interior

The interior seemed out of this world. The rear compartment featured a large, heavily-upholstered, L-shaped Chesterfield-style couch. Front occupants were greeted by a total absence of dashboard or instrument panel: the controls were mounted discreetly by the driver on the side of the cabin, with one round instrument near the base of the windscreen. Apart from the steering wheel, the vehicle appeared, at first glance, to be controlled by thought transference, as one by now might expect.

What happened next?

It appears that three Brubaker Boxes were built, originally. The prototype featured in a film, and another version was used in a TV science fiction series. The enterprise folded when Volkswagen decided it wouldn't sell Brubaker Beetle platforms.

Conspiracy theorists no doubt imagined 'Men in Black' being deployed to try and clean up this unfortunate space/time aberration. However, up until around 1979, various bodyshops managed to produce a few more Boxes, primarily 50 Automecca 'Sports Vans' – renamed, some might say, in an attempt to confuse the authorities.

Research reveals some examples surviving in remote, rural corners of the States. Recent attempts to access sites previously claiming to possess the body

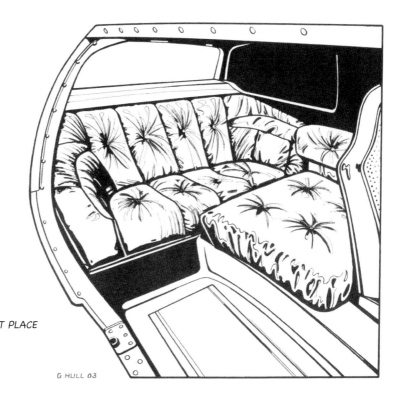

THE REAR, L-SHAPED CHESTERFIELD SOFA WAS A TYPICALLY PROVOCATIVE, NON-DETROIT APPROACH. CALIFORNIANS OBSERVED: 'GREAT PLACE FOR A PARTY!'

G HULL 03

moulds have been rewarded with a 'This domain has expired' notice. However, diligent investigation led to the discovery of a rare original brochure being sold in America, which is now safely in the UK.

Summary

Brubaker had anticipated so many trends, that, to regard him as just an average kind of guy from the Los Angeles Art Center College of Design, as claimed, seems simplistic. It's hard to think of any other vehicles that have got closer to the following decade's design trends and philosophy.

The Box had the ultimate, cab-forward look, and is certainly in the Sports Utility or Minivan territory before these even existed. The Box was a recreational vehicle, and, by definition, a lifestyle statement, well before anyone even knew what MPV stood for (Multi Purpose Vehicle). The proportions and 'wheel awareness' bring to mind Hummers, and the rear aspect a BMW X3 or X5.

Apparently, Brubaker was involved with the Learjet executive aircraft design, and worked briefly in GM's advanced studios before going independent. Search engines discover Curtis Brubaker in Los Angeles as a successful designer/entrepreneur, and, by the late 1990s, our hero appears to have been involved in applied electronics and various patents. In 2014, Curtis broke cover, and during a phone interview in the USA, spoke enthusiastically to the journalist about the Box's Premium Sports Van approach still being valid. To quote the man: "Most modern cars have too much s*** going on" – that simplicity is the hardest thing to get right, but it's always the best path. He mentioned being involved with Tesla and Ford, perhaps to find another suitable chassis/platform with which to display some new ideas.

Conclusion

It may be that Curtis Brubaker was simply a regular ex-GM designer who had a flash of inspiration as the 1960s met the 70s. But it's equally intriguing to imagine a shape-shifting alien life form jumping the fence at Roswell Army Air Field on a wild night in 1947, a survivor, perhaps, of the crashed UFO rumoured to have been secreted away there ...

One of the original investors was described by Brubaker as becoming "unruly."

Owners admitted inadvertently causing accidents among startled observers, and, due to this, one resorted to only driving his at night. Mind you, seeing this unearthly presence on a remote country road at night might not be so calming for the nerves, either.

THE BABY LAMBORGHINI – BRAVO

1974

BRAVO'S UNIQUE TWISTING TOP SURFACE UNITES HORIZONTAL FRONT AND REAR WITH ANGLED CABIN SIDES. HEADLAMPS, WIPERS, AND AIR DUCTS ARE CONCEALED WITHIN AN ARCHITECTURAL GRID.

BELLA MACCHINA!

"Bravo's style embodies something of the prophet's soothsaying, pointing to the pose of an unidentified moving object of the future." This was how a Japanese design publication attempted to sum up the Lamborghini Bravo. Makes you think, doesn't it? ... But let's start at the beginning.

Background

Whilst Ferraris were based on a legendary history of racing and wonderfully shaped bodies, Lamborghini was a late, 'bull-in-a-china-shop' arrival. Of course, its bull badge was the perfect, politically incorrect symbol for this new, rather raw and headstrong, but wealthy, member of the Italian motoring scene.

Lamborghini's first offerings – 1964's 350GT and 1966's 400GT 2+2 – were typical of numerous contemporary Italian coachbuilders, and possibly what you might expect from a car enthusiast who'd made his money in tractors, industrial and domestic heaters, and air-conditioning equipment. Ferruccio Lamborghini had a thing about taking on Ferrari, and hired engineers who had worked for that company, but it all began to get really interesting when he teamed up with Bertone Design, arguably second only to Pininfarina as a design consultant, the latter being associated with Ferrari ...

At the 1965 Turin Motor Show, upstart Lamborghini caused a sensation by showing a chassis made from steel box-sections, instead of traditional tubing, and flaunting a transverse mid-engine 350bhp V12 – a first for any road car. By 1966, this chassis was shown clothed in a stunning suit, tailored by Bertone's Marcello Gandini. This direct and credible challenge to Ferrari was named after a breed of fighting bull, the Miura.

Several interesting cars from the Lamborghini factory at Sant'Agata Bolognese followed, but the Miura was a tough act to follow. Then came something that *did* challenge the Miura: and which was, for some, was the most exciting sports car ever; a genuine supercar – the Lamborghini Countach.

Shown for the first time in early 1971, customers had to wait until 1974 to get their hands on one. Famous for its raised 'insect wing' doors, other-worldly appearance, and fearsome performance, the Countach was the epitome of Italian machismo. The show car of 1971 was an original and sophisticated shape, again by Miura man Gandini at Bertone. It soon had to grow protruding air-scoop 'ears' to cool the big 375bhp mid-mounted engine, but the trouble was it kept growing these add-on appendages all over the car, until it reached its final stage of automotive pornography: the iconic poster of the Countach, displayed on many a schoolboy's bedroom wall.

This pumped-up, muscle-bound monster must have made Gandini wince, but some like their meat rare/raw, and anyway 'Countach' was a suitably dramatic Italian exclamation.

Whilst acknowledging the appeal of Ferraris, Lamborghinis have been a touch more extraordinary, rarer, and extreme. Watching Miuras and the intimidating Countachs shrieking around London's South Kensington in the 1960s and '70s, their potency, undiluted emotion, exclusivity and undeniable sense of occasion was memorable.

So, how to follow that, and make something that mere mortals could aspire to?

Enter the Bravo, another fighting bull (Bertone Studio Project 114)

By definition, Bravo was always going to be exceptional as it was the first attempt to make a 'Baby Lamborghini.' Designed by the same hand that created the legendary and charismatic Miura and Countach, Bertone's Marcello Gandini, the end result was never going to be boring.

Discovering the Bravo at the 1974 Turin Motor Show, it took a while for this observer to absorb this radical newcomer. This was a new, smaller Lamborghini that looked like nothing on earth. Climbing in over the widest sill in the world, negotiating the outrageously intrusive front wheel box, finally snuggling down behind the small thick-rimmed steering wheel and looking through the radical windscreen and side glasses, you entered another world – that of the supercar. No longer a bystander, but a player, sitting in a chariot of the Gods, but one that mere mortals could relate to. Surely not? Well, almost, but maybe the Gods resented it, for, as fate had it, the Bravo never went into production.

Mechanicals

The Bravo was based on the 1970 Urraco 2+2 platform, cut in two, shortened by 8in (203mm), and a new body welded on. The Italians are great at this sort of impromptu engineering, and the result was driven to the show with the snap-crackle-and-pop you'd expect. Powered by the transverse 250bhp, three-litre V8, it was as wide as a Countach at 74in (1880mm), 16in (406mm) shorter, and a shade lower at 40.7in (1034mm). At 2392lb (1085kg) the Bravo was 628lb (285kg) lighter than a L400 Countach.

Because it was mechanically a cut-and-shut Urraco, the Bravo was a viable road car, and this prototype did at least 40,000 miles of testing, including by Chief Test Driver Bob Wallace, and

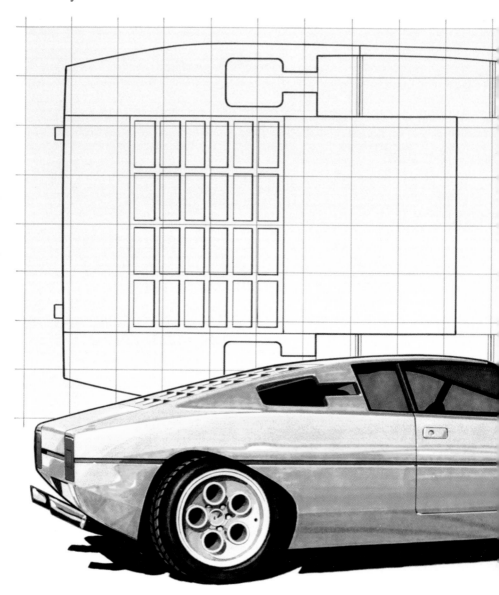

was good for over 165mph. The 15in (381mm) wheels were considerably wider on the rear than the front – normal practice for this sort of projectile.

Bravo's styling design
Aesthetically fascinating to followers of automotive fashion, the Bravo was much featured in publications, and shown photographed from every conceivable angle. A Japanese book on Bertone featured a Bravo on the cover – the ultimate accolade. The Countach's looks had been a shock, and its sibling offered no respite in challenging conventional beauty or assumptions about what a sports car should look like. Whereas, to many eyes, an E-Type

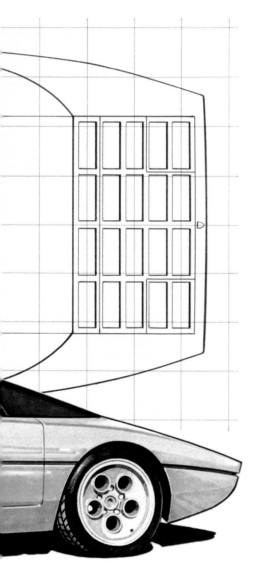

G.HULL 03

1974: MODERN ARCHITECTURE MEETS AUTOMOTIVE MACHINE. THE LAMBORGHINI BRAVO CHALLENGED PRECONCEPTIONS OF WHAT A SPORTS CAR SHOULD LOOK LIKE – ITALIAN VISUAL AUTHORITY AT ITS BEST.

in the later, bespoiled stage, flaunting its potency with all that visual noise – dogs who bark a lot are not always the most dangerous. With Bravo, even when parked on the Motor Show stand, you could almost hear the exhaust system cracking and banging as it cooled after a manic drive. Although it looked extraordinary, it was, at the same time, self-contained and understated, making it both convincing and desirable.

Gandini was wilfully pushing styling design's visual envelope, particularly with regard to glass treatment: even the feed-in to the engine's recessed side air scoops were glass. The submerged, sharply-raked windscreen pillars were positioned well inboard, and, combined with the unusual side glass treatment, created the illusion of a large wraparound screen. This beguiling glass area allowed the upper body side to roll, uniquely, from horizontal at the nose through 45 degrees to form the cabin, and back to horizontal at the rear – a very daring visual ploy, but expertly executed.

Although the doors opened conventionally, the Countach-influenced rear wheelarch shape remained wilfully provocative. A distinctive, black groove ran round the car, tying together the mismatched wheelarches, and front and rear lights helped form an harmonious whole ... which the Countach lacked.

Headlamps, wipers and air-vents were concealed under a large architectural-type modular grid (or, if you don't like the grid, 'storm drain') rather than a conventional bonnet. This grid was echoed at the rear, completely concealing the rear glass. The roof panel was the

Jaguar, for instance, is beautiful, the Bravo projected a more elusive appeal. Avoiding overt sculpturing, spoilers and power bulges, it exuded obsessive purpose. There is an air of understated menace; a bit like Michael Caine's performance in *Get Carter*, it's all about subtle body language.

Some feel the Countach lost the plot

same width as the bonnet and 'boot' panels, driving two parallel lines from front to back. When seen in plan view, the effect was more like a two-dimensional graphic: no wonder the Japanese considered that it was 'pointing to the pose of an unidentified moving object of the future.' The shape simply defies categorisation.

For alloy wheel-spotters, this was the first sighting of Lamborghini's superb 'five-cylinder' style. When a new car style appears, there's an irresistible urge among some to try and find comparisons and influences. Comparisons are odious, and achieve little apart from generating irritation, but, still, fools rush in, so let's have a go.

The most common comparison with the Bravo is Gandini's 1971 Lancia Stratos. Again a compact, transverse mid-engined chariot that used a distinctive glass area feature to aesthetic effect, and generally from the same gene pool as Gandini's 1974 offspring.

However, the Stratos is visually quite cluttered-looking – even before its rallying accoutrements were added. The Stratos is very good; the Bravo is better.

Perhaps a more pertinent comparison is the Lotus Esprit, launched in 1975, but first seen in 1972 as an Italdesign concept by Giorgetto Giugiaro: two shapes answering a similar design brief at a similar point in time. The Esprit is a desirable sports car, stylistically created from very simple, folded flat planes, as in origami. The flat, sharply-raked windscreen is very much of its time.

Giugiaro is rightly regarded as a master of design. The Bravo seems to have broken away from the shackles of evolution, and is speaking in a new language of aesthetic sophistication. The Bravo has no chinks in its body armour; the Esprit does: from the rear it just looks too wide. Strangely, the superb and much

later 1990 Honda NSX suffers from the same 'broad beam' syndrome, which the Bravo avoids by tucking in its rear wings at the last possible moment.

Interior
The Bravo's interior made little attempt to impress, but was refreshingly uncluttered. The simple, padded, flat-board fascia carried a series of 'fretwork' instrument cut-outs, apparently influenced by the exterior air intake shapes, immediately behind the side glass. The then new Alcantara artificial, suede-type material was used on the seats and some trim areas; this soft and warm material soon became very popular.

In total
To sum up, this car appeals on several levels. Not just an exotic pedigree with breathtaking dynamics, and not just an exciting form study, the Bravo is a mixture of all three, which conjures up powerful magic; the kind that slightly unhinges people, including this still-open-mouthed bystander. Concept cars come and go: some good, some not so good. The Bravo was very special.

What happened next?
Unfortunately, Bravo's almost supernatural presence couldn't protect it from the worldwide economic downturn and oil crisis of the seventies, which branded any such vehicle frivolous. The Company's dynamo Ferruccio Lamborghini sold the firm in 1974, and retired. Bankrupted in 1978, it was bought out of receivership in 1984 and sold on to the Chrysler Corporation in 1987, then sold again in 1994, eventually being bought by VW in 1998.

Despite these lurid circumstances, it's rumoured that the Bravo was still being considered for production in 1978, and then wheeled out again for review under Chrysler management in the late 1980s.

It would've been hard to believe in 1974 that, one day in the future, yours truly would be invited to Sant'Agata to look around and drive a Diablo (not the most relaxing car). On my visit in 1998, however, enquiries at the factory about the Bravo, and also at Bertone, drew a blank. The Lamborghini that had been begging to go into production had been 'disappeared.'

Gandini's masterpiece eventually reappeared in Bertone's museum, and was sold in 2011 as part of that design firm's eventual demise. Tellingly, it was said to be the only exhibit refurbished for the sale: originally shown in metallic gold and then green, it went out in shimmering pearlescent white with its head held high. It was sold to a collector for £511,000 – over twice the estimate. Actions speak louder than words.

It's a great shame that the Bravo was not to be, as motoring enthusiasts have been denied its assured, charismatic, presence on the world's automotive and artistic stages. However, the great idea of a 'Baby Lambo' persisted, and, with VW resources, the 2003 Gallardo made its entrance; Lamborghini sold 14,022 example – its most successful model.

I guess the Bravo's light never quite went out ...

The Bravo introduced one of the all-time great alloy wheel designs. Today's super low-profile tyres have led to very large diameter wheels, with often skeletal spokes to flaunt the brakes (and often bits of suspension), with their gaudily-painted callipers. The overall effect is like looking at a too-explicit illustration in a medical textbook. The Bravo's wheel implies there is something interesting going on behind it, but no need to look too deeply.

They say you have to hand-wash a car before you really get to know its shape, and even better in this respect is to make a 'one-off' scale model. When finished, you'll possess great knowledge, but will also have become just a little deranged in the process.

The Bravo prototype's three changes of paint hue is not unusual: colour is so fundamental. If a flying black beetle lands on a child (and some adults) the child may run round in circles screaming, but a ladybird's partially red wing covers get a completely different reaction.

TYRRELL P34
SIX-WHEELER

1975-1977

THE FOUR-WHEELED FRONT
BOGIE OF TYRRELL'S 1975
P34 FLEW IN THE FACE OF
TRADITION. THIS IS THE
LATER, MORE AERODYNAMIC,
BODY. LACK OF TYRE
DEVELOPMENT REMAINED A
MAJOR PROBLEM.

HOW MANY WHEELS?!

It's hard to imagine going much more boldly than designer Derek Gardner's Tyrrell P34 six-wheeler Formula One car, a contender for the most surprising, distinctive – not to say eccentric – racing car design ever. Unveiled in September 1975, it's not hard to see why it simply stunned the 'seen it all' motoring scribes.

Background

Although tempting to wax lyrical about this revolutionary, crowd-pleasing device, we have to remember that top level motorsport has little room for flights of fancy. So what was Derek Gardner up to? Well, motorsport is all

about doing what you have to do to win, and, in Gardner's words, he was seeking an 'unfair advantage.' Like his contemporaries, he was frustrated by a level playing field. Most of the top teams were using Ford Cosworth DFV 465bhp engines, Hewland gearboxes, and the same tyres, so how to steal a march on this evenly-balanced pack?

Gardner was looking for a 50bhp advantage, and, to understand his reasons for using four front wheels, we have to try and see the perceived advantages through the logical eyes of an F1 designer.

Aerodynamics:
F1 regulations fixed nose height to front wheel rim height; thus, smaller wheels

allowed a lower, more aerodynamic, nose. The 10in (253mm) wheel and tyre was 4in (100mm) lower than the standard 13in (330mm) offering. A spinning, exposed wheel generates lift relative to its diameter: smaller wheels create less lift, thus increasing downforce, and more downforce requires less power-absorbing front wing. This factor has been cited as a key incentive behind the P34, and 13in (330mm) front wheels contributed 12% of total drag on the previous 007 Elf-Tyrrell, so, reducing wheel diameter reduces drag.

Braking:
Two additional front brakes gave 34% greater swept disc area, and 10in (253mm) wheels spin 30% faster than conventional 13in (330mm) ones, thereby allowing greater brake cooling.

Handling:
There was 40% greater front tyre contact area, resulting in excellent 1.88g cornering. The four-wheel setup increased steering effort by just 10-15%.

Weight:
Due to smaller front components, only a 33lb (15kg) weight penalty was incurred (11cwt (575kg) total vehicle weight).

Safety:
Four wheels allowed superior steering and braking control if a front tyre punctured.

Did it work?
With all of these apparent advantages, the obvious question is: was this radical approach any good? Well, we shouldn't be surprised that the answer isn't that straightforward. During the 1976 and 1977 seasons, when P34 was raced, the following downsides became evident:

Aerodynamics:
There is a common misconception that

P34 was about better aerodynamic penetration and lower drag, due to the low nose and narrow front track (45.6in (1160mm); rear 59in (1500mm). But, as Gardner knew, most drag is caused by how much the air is disrupted at the rear, and, in this respect, the Tyrrell was conventional – although rear track was reduced by 3in (76mm), the tyres were a little wider than previously. The real drag damage was created by the Tyrell's huge rear tyres and wing, just as on its rivals, so little advantage was gained there.

For the 1977 season the P34B had cleaner aerodynamics, and Kevlar replaced the fibreglass body, but the vehicle was wider and heavier.

Braking:
On less-than-smooth surfaces the lighter loaded front tyres could be unpredictable regarding lock-up. Apart from anything else, if one of the tandem front wheels locked, it effectively changed the wheelbase, and thus the handling. The conventionally-sized front wheels used by everyone else allowed bigger diameter brakes, which also benefited from ongoing development, thereby reducing Tyrrell's advantage.

P34, in its two seasons, suffered from overheating front brakes. 'Periscope' ducts were tried for the rear set of front brakes, but obviously they increased drag and weight.

Handling:
The front 'train-bogie'-like layout required careful set-up, ie spring rates, dampers, anti-roll bar, tyre pressures, toe-in/out, camber and castor became very precise, further complicated by certain conditions provoking the aforementioned wheelbase fluctuations. The wheelbase, measured from the front wheels, was 6in (152mm) shorter than 007's, presumably to save weight.

Tyres:

The unique, small, front tyre compound and structure were the P34's Achilles' heel. The problem was commercial rather than design: Tyrrell simply didn't have the clout to persuade Goodyear, the supplier, to put huge effort into just one team's limited call-off quantity.

All of the other teams, sharing tyre design, benefited from ongoing development, and Tyrrell's roller-skate fronts became the Cinderella of the ball. Tyrrell, of course, shared the rear tyre improvements with the other teams, which added to an increasing discrepancy, front to rear. A further complication that compounded the tyre's specification was that the lighter loaded front tyres ran cooler, requiring a different compound to achieve optimum working temperature.

Initially, drivers were disconcerted that they couldn't see what the front wheels were doing. Windows were cut into the P34's 'conning tower' cockpit sides, but, psychologically, this might have been a mixed blessing, as at 180mph the tyres were rotating at considerably over 3000rpm. The associated centrifugal force at these revs caused distortion of the side-wall not encountered with the slower rotating rears.

Grand Prix achievements

Notwithstanding the preceding analysis, P34 did work ... mostly. Many maintain that the 1970s were a golden age for F1, with Jackie Stewart, Niki Lauda, James Hunt, Jody Scheckter, etc, driving Ferraris, McLarens, Tyrrells and Brabhams. Jody Scheckter, Patrick Depailler and Ronnie Peterson were the drivers associated with P34.

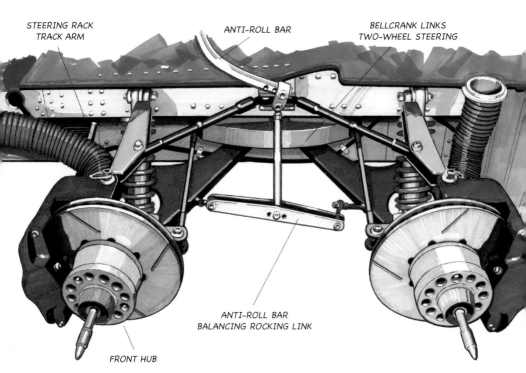

STEERING RACK TRACK ARM — ANTI-ROLL BAR — BELLCRANK LINKS TWO-WHEEL STEERING — ANTI-ROLL BAR BALANCING ROCKING LINK — FRONT HUB

NOT AS COMPLICATED AS IT FIRST APPEARS: TWO EXTRA BRAKES, TWO EXTRA WHEELS TO STEER WITH, SMALLER FRONTAL AREA, AND CONTROLLABLE IF A TYRE PUNCTURES, COMPENSATING FOR SLIGHTLY INCREASED WEIGHT AND STEERING EFFORT.

INITIALLY SUCCESSFUL, JODY SCHECKTER AND PATRICK DEPAILLER CAME 1ST AND 2ND IN THE 1976 SWEDISH GRAND PRIX, BUT TYRRELL COULDN'T SHARE THE OTHER TEAM'S TYRE DEVELOPMENT. COCKPIT SIDE WINDOWS ALLOWED DRIVERS TO COUNT THE WHEELS.

In the 1976 Swedish Grand Prix, Sheckter and Depailler came first and second in the six-wheeler's fourth race, with Niki Lauda's Ferrari a distant third. During the 1976 season, in 13 races, P34 drivers achieved ten podium places, Scheckter and Depailler finishing third and fourth behind world champions James Hunt (McLaren), and Niki Lauda (Ferrari). The Tyrrell set three fastest laps, and was third in the Constructors' Championship.

It should also be pointed out that, in late December 1976, at the Paul Ricard circuit, Patrick Depailler bettered the F1 lap record by one second. The six-wheeler had the most successful inaugural year in F1 of any car or team.

In 1977, as the Elf-Tyrrell's technical advantage was whittled away, one second and three third places were achieved. By the 1978 season Tyrrell was back to just four wheels.

Conclusions
Initially, Derek Gardner's multi-wheeled brainwave had an advantage over its four-

wheeled rivals. But the conventional cars were able to share ongoing developments, particularly in tyres, that the Tyrrell's unique front tyres were denied. On a smooth track the P34 had exceptional turn-in ability on corners, and stability under braking. Jody Scheckter seems to have had a love-hate relationship with this design. He thought the front tyres locked-up too easily: "If we'd had ABS [Anti-lock Braking System] at that time, it would have been fantastic."

Ultimately, one has to acknowledge that the four-wheel 'train bogie' was heavier than a conventional layout, and that front tyre issues and brakes overheating couldn't be resolved in the time available.

However, we mustn't forget that motor racing is a spectator sport, and spectators loved this novel device. It was different, and you could see the driver's hands at work through the side windows.

Postscript
In 2000 with Gardner's involvement,

To Boldly Go

a 1977 specification P34 won the thoroughbred Grand Prix Championship on specially-developed Avon tyres, beating the more recent ground-effect cars pioneered by Lotus (ground-effect being inverted aerofoils in side pods that sucked the car down on the ground).

It's tempting to indulge in conjecture about further four-front-wheeled F1 cars using modern tyres, smaller rear tyres, carbon fibre, adjustable aerodynamics, and electronic aids. The spectacle of a couple of competitive, hard-charging six-wheelers would again enrich the phenomenon that is Formula One.

Jody Scheckter: "I never agreed with the fundamental concepts behind it. It worked on smooth surfaces but, back then, there weren't many of those around. But it was massively controllable. You could do anything with that car. And if you got into trouble you could get out of it instantly."

Scheckter once pulled into the pits after losing a front wheel, and to amuse his mechanics just complained of understeer.

Intriguingly, Jackie Stewart, who had retired from motor racing after winning the 1973 World Championship for Elf Team Tyrrell, tried the P34 shortly after it was launched. Known for choosing his words, he commented that it felt no heavier to steer, and potentially very good.

The benefit to sponsors of TV camera time shouldn't be underestimated. One team apparently allowed its no-chance F1 entrant to run out of fuel just to secure some coverage.

ALFA ROMEO SZ

1989-1991

EMPLOYING ARTISTIC LICENCE, THIS FRONT THREE-QUARTER VIEW OF THE ALFA ROMEO 1989 SZ IS ITS BEST, PARTICULARLY THE NOSE AND HEADLAMP ARRANGEMENT. THE CHALLENGING OVERALL STYLE CLOTHED DYNAMIC EXCELLENCE.

'IL MOSTRO'

"**U**gly, ghastly, ridiculous, monstrous," said *CAR* magazine. The Italian press called it 'Il Mostro' (The Monster). Rarely-rattled *Autocar* said, "completely mad Zagato styling." An acclaimed international car designer indulged in a ranting, vitriolic condemnation of it in *Design* magazine. It's rare for a car's appearance to be so vilified, but Alfa's SZ was universally panned. So why doesn't this observer also condemn it? Well, there really is more to this car than meets the eye, which tends to force one to stop and consider just what a true sports car is.

Background
SZ (Sprint Zagato)/ ES-30
(Experimental Sports car 3-litre)

By the late 1980s, Fiat and Alfa Romeo were struggling with a tarnished image of poor quality generally. Alfa was near bankruptcy, and Zagato was tending to move into other fields of industrial work. All parties needed a pick-me-up, and it appears they decided to cooperate on a supercoupé concept.

This controversial coupé's conception and birth seem a little complicated, but rapid. Sketches to launch at the 1989 Geneva Motor Show took just 19 months with the use if Computer Aided Design (CAD) and machining (CAM). Although described as a Zagato

To Boldly Go

concept ES-30, in 1987 three design teams contributed, combining the considerable talents of Alfa Romeo, Fiat and Zagato. Several individuals are mentioned – Robert Opron and Mario Maioli of Fiat, for example, and Alfa Romeo's Walter da Silva. Antonio Castellana of Fiat is credited as having finalised exterior and interior styling. SZ was essentially a concept car that made it into production.

The coupé was produced between 1989 and 1991, and as the RZ convertible from 1992 to 1994. Around 1036 SZs were built, including several prototypes and 278 convertibles. People enjoy driving this honest, red-blooded Italian sports car, which has none of the modern driver aids. Good for short or long journeys, they're all left-hand drive.

Mechanicals

In engineering terms, the car ticked all the boxes, and then some. Mechanically based on the Alfa Romeo 75 platform wheelbase of 98.8in (2509mm), and employing its 3.0-litre, V6, 210bhp-tuned engine and rear-mounted transaxle, it delivered a top speed of 153mph with a 0-60mph time of 6.9 seconds, so no sluggard. The vehicle weighed 2769lb (1256kg).

The Alfa 75 suspension was modified by the Lancia and Fiat works rally team manager, with knowledge gleaned from racing 75s. This included the surprisingly sophisticated addition of Koni hydraulic adjustable height suspension, enabling SZs to be lowered by 2in (50mm) to give just 3.2in (80mm) ground clearance. This extreme setting, coupled with special Pirelli P6 asymmetric tyres, resulted in exceptional cornering ability: 1.4g apparently being recorded.

Despite major reservations about the car's appearance, *Autocar* rated it as one of the greatest cars it'd ever driven;

an example of this vehicle's perverse personality.

Body

Body construction – a steel monocoque with bonded, injection-moulded, glass-fibre reinforced resin composite exterior panels, aluminium roof panel and carbon-fibre spoiler – was no less promising than performance, and created a very rigid structure, no doubt helping handling and ride.

The distinctive, visually-divorced superstructure included wide integral door window frames. The gap lines on the roof are quite narrow compared to those on the lower body, which, in some cases, are wide enough to be considered a design feature.

THE UNCOMFORTABLE SURFACES, DIVIDED BY SAVAGE PANEL JOINTS, DISTRACTED FROM JUST HOW NEAR THE GROUND THE SZ COULD GET. ADJUSTABLE SUSPENSION AND ASYMMETRIC PIRELLI TYRES ENABLED IT TO PULL 1.4g ... AND IT DID HAVE GREAT WHEELS.

Wind tunnel work ensured good downforce, and a very respectable coefficient of drag figure of Cd 0.3. Body shape appears to follow all the correct aerodynamic rules to give speed and stability, ie, deep front apron, low nose, high scuttle (base of windscreen), well curved and narrow windscreen, high tail with additional boot spoiler, and sharply cut off rear end. The feed-in from the top of the windscreen to the roof in particular is textbook airflow management.

'Chilli Red' was the only paint colour permitted, with a dark grey roof and spoiler.

SZ was 160in (4064mm) long, 68in (1727mm) wide, and not particularly low at 51.6in (1311mm).

Exterior appearance or, er, 'Style'

Well, I guess we have to return to the elephant in the room: the car's appearance. To be kind, the chosen 'aesthetic' is aggressive/brutal; to be unkind it's like a boxer who's had several fights too many, a scaled-up child's toy, a novelty birthday cake for a six-year-old. Even through rose-tinted glasses, the SZ is not a pretty sight; indeed, some would prefer to look at bag ladies dancing the Can-Can or a Scotsman doing handstands. From first visual contact to final baffled disengagement, aesthetic confusion reigns.

At the risk of succumbing to cliché, the front of this car really doesn't look like it belongs to the back. It's not

GH.15

even an arranged marriage between the two, but rather a shotgun wedding with neither party happy. The unholy union irredeemably collapses where the unthinking bonnet shut lines chop down into the front wheelarch. The door panel looks as if it wishes it were anywhere but at the scene of the crime.

Considering its pedigree, the body style just doesn't seem to have been professionally resolved. There is mention of it being the result of an early computer design machining programme, ie, feeding coordinates from a promising sketch or scale model to a computer-controlled milling cutter. This robotically cuts the shape into a block of something solid; usually clay.

SZ does have the look of a scale model that has been digitally enlarged or copy-milled to full size. Such procedures are very quick, but invariably require a period of hand-working by artisans to finesse surface subtleties. The surfacing, which should ensure smooth reflection of light,

is not perfect, although, perversely, this tends to at least distract from some of the lumpen features.

Its visually separate superstructure is, coincidentally, very similar in concept to the contemporary, and admired, 1990 Honda NSX. But, unlike the Honda, it sits on a relatively narrow, boxy, high-tailed body. The front end appears to have been trodden on, then softened independently to the rear end's abandoned cubist expression. Some cars look generally pretty good, but perhaps have a weak aspect from a certain angle, an Achilles' heel, but SZ *is* an Achilles' heel. It simply looks wrong in the round ... although front three-quarters through a telephoto lens is borderline acceptable.

The headlamp treatment for 1987 has to be applauded for its sheer audacity, probably influenced by availability and avoidance of tooling costs. Nevertheless, setting those jewel-like clusters in the narrow slot adjacent to the vestigial Alfa radiator motif is a nice touch.

SZ'S REAR VIEW RATTLES EVEN DEVOTEES, IT DOESN'T MATCH THE FRONT. YET, HOWEVER AWKWARD THE BRUTALLY-CURTAILED TAIL, AERODYNAMICALLY IT'S GOOD. THE 'SEPARATE' ROOF IS SIMILAR TO THAT OF THE HONDA NSX.

Unfortunately, compared to what's happening at the rear end, this delicate touch is synonymous with a knuckle-scraping bouncer wearing a diamond tie pin.

The front and rear side lamps have smoked lenses. The front lamps live in the previously-mentioned headlamp slot, but, at the rear, the similarly proportioned slim lamp belt unfortunately draws attention to the adjacent flat body slabs, which are reminiscent of those cast by shuttered concrete on a building site.

Strangely enough, the bolted-rim 16in (406mm) alloy wheels are as good as any you'll ever see, but with their super low-profile tyres, they appear embarrassed to be supporting this 'lacking in social graces' bodywork. If ever a car was entitled to shrug its shoulders, this is it ...

Interior style

For a vehicle that was intended as something of a low production stop-gap, the interior is rather good. You are immediately struck by two tan 'orthopaedic'-type bucket seats, featuring massive cushion and backrest side bolster protrusions to steady you against significant cornering forces. Being a driver's car, the fascia is quite rightly biased towards the steering wheel, with nothing to distract the passenger from preparing themself, as best they can, for the inevitable next bend. The door trim pads shamelessly reflect the subtlety of the car's exterior, although there is a grab handle, at least.

Conclusion

Cars, like people, portray a certain body language, and I wouldn't want to share a police cell with this example. Oh, but, but, but, it's the antithesis of the dreaded hairdresser car syndrome: a wild wedge, its backside stuck up in the air, it's a beady-eyed Desperate Dan looking for trouble. Gunslingers don't need social skills; this spaghetti western is Italian machismo in the raw, and it's just too bad if you don't like red meat. All actors want to play the villain, and I suspect Alfa's SZ is not short of guilty fans ... just like this one.

> This is a car that challenges, and asks questions such as, 'Who are you looking at?!'

DELTAWING

2012 on

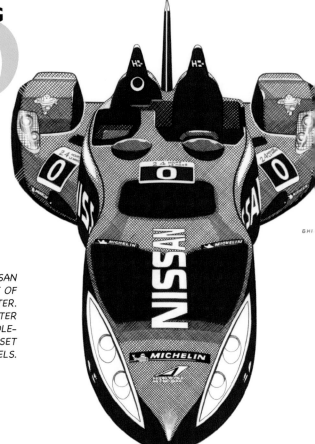

BEN BOWLBY'S 2012 'NISSAN DELTAWING' IS REMINISCENT OF AN EARTH-BOUND JET FIGHTER. WITH A REAR WIDTH GREATER THAN A BENTLEY'S, ITS NEEDLE-NOSE HOUSES VERY CLOSE-SET NARROW WHEELS.

SOMETIMES IT'S WORTH DOING THINGS BY HALF

Despite the exotic cutting-edge image of racing cars, most have evolved in a pretty conventional manner. Breakthroughs have occurred, such as the birdcage chassis, disc brakes, mid-engine, composites, and so on, but it is generally incremental, linear stuff. Big, progressive advances have not always been encouraged or adopted when they did occur, often falling foul of the racing establishment's regulations. Club racing has traditionally been the place for experimentation, where sponsorship money doesn't make it

inevitable that teams will violently object to any other team's perceived 'unfair advantage.'

It's a truism that racing, if not actually about cheating, is about studying regulations to determine what can be gotten away with, a classic example being the total ban on adjusting the aerodynamics of F1 cars while in motion, although some bright spark realised it was possible to influence airflow over the rear wing by the driver moving his body. Once the hysteria had died down, all were soon allowed to have adjustable rear wings to some degree, and in certain race circumstances.

The DeltaWing project is a member of that very small club of vehicle design where all conventional wisdom has been put on hold, and a racing car is genuinely designed starting with a clean sheet of paper, with existing cars used only as a template to challenge.

Background

In 2008 British designer Ben Bowlby began to consider a new concept for the American IndyCar Series. Traditionally, racing car designers seek to achieve maximum performance by juggling the three elements of weight, power, and aerodynamics. Conventional wisdom quite reasonably assumes that, within regulations and classes, excellent power-to-weight ratio with good aerodynamics equals a potential winner. In this situation, best practice suspension, tyres and brakes are a given, as everyone uses similar components anyway, and also, of course, a good driver.

This 'comfort zone' situation can be a little stultifying as participants tend to nuance designs rather than make rapid evolutionary progress. If, however, as Ben Bowlby appears to have done, one allows some elements to radically skew the power/weight/aerodynamic dynamic, the 'comfort zone' of conventional wisdom is challenged.

In this case, the wild card in question was fuel efficiency, with the moral not to rely on the greedy God power, but to attack weight and enhance airflow management to gauge how little energy is required in order to win. By upsetting the apple cart in this manner, the resulting design will at least be interesting, and possibly more relevant to man's overall progress.

The so-called DeltaWing was unveiled in 2010: a very unconventional wheeled vehicle – an open two-seater with a very wide rear track, semi-exposed rear wheels, and a tail fin – looking like nothing on earth, other than, possibly, an earthbound Concorde.

The body narrowed tightly by the cockpit into a long, pointed fuselage, bizarrely supported by two, semi-exposed, very narrow-track front wheels.

In mid-2010 the design was rejected by IndyCar, but a year later was accepted as a 'Garage 56' (experimental) entrant for the 2012 24-hour Le Mans. Early in 2012, Nissan came on board with an engine in return for naming rights. Thus, the project became the Nissan DeltaWing.

Like all good ideas it is quite, well, clever

Ben Bowlby's design solutions were so radical it's difficult to follow his original creative process without being similarly gifted, so we'll simply consider the car's basic premise.

If a racing car's weight is halved, and likewise the power required, fuel consumption and tyre wear will also be halved. At the same time, dramatically improved aerodynamics will result in a vehicle that will not only keep up with the opposition, but should be a little faster all-round.

Mechanicals

A 1600cc, 300bhp, direct injection, four-cylinder turbo engine was prepared by Ray Mallock (UK). The vehicle was mid-engined, the block in-line with the chassis, and gearbox and final drive at the rear. This relatively small engine required only 55% of the benchmark V8 Nissan engine's fuel, thus allowing a smaller fuel tank.

- At 183in (4650mm), the DeltaWing's length is similar to a medium-sized saloon car.
- Its 78.74in (2000mm) width is greater

G.H I3

REJECTING DRAG-INDUCING AIRFLOW APPENDAGES TO CREATE DOWNFORCE, IN FAVOUR OF A CLEVERLY-SHAPED UNDERSIDE, THE DELTAWING COULD EMPLOY A SMALLER, FUEL-EFFICIENT ENGINE.

than a Bentley Arnage body.

- Front track is only 24in (610mm). The tyres are 4in (100mm) wide, similar to a Citroën 2CV. According to the designer, these close-coupled tyres share cornering loads equally, unlike conventional set-ups, where the outside tyre loads-up, and tends to understeer. The steering is very light and fast. Wheels are 15in (381mm).
- The vehicle weighs 9.35cwt (475kg), with 72.5% of weight over the rear wheels. This rear bias gives excellent traction, and, because of the low overall weight, tyre wear is reduced, necessitating fewer pit stops.
- All roll-stiffness is at the rear, aided by a very sophisticated variable damping system.
- With only 27.5% of the already very light vehicle weight being on the front wheels, all front components,

suspension, steering and brakes can also be lighter.

- Because a light car is easier to stop, the braking system is only about half the usual weight. Most of the DeltaWing's braking occurs at the rear; this gives 'parachute stability,' because even if the rear wheels lock, there isn't the tendency for the car to spin, as in a conventional layout. Again, due to reduced braking loads at the front, the local structure can be lighter.

Body

- The general chassis/body is a typical bonded composite 'monocoque.' Its dual purpose is to locate components and to achieve the designer's unique delta-wing aerodynamics.
- Its aerodynamic coefficient of drag (Cd) is 0.35. This is on the low side

for competition cars, which, typically, rely on drag-inducing appendages to create downforce, and then have to use brute power to force the high-drag edifice through the air. The smooth DeltaWing has all its downforce generated by the underside. 76% of all its downforce is at the rear. Moveable 'Gurney Flap' trim-tabs on the trailing edges of the delta-wing were allowed on experimental cars.

• Intriguingly, despite rearward bias of downforce and weight, directional stability doesn't appear to be an issue.

The mechanicals and body combine to achieve a top speed of 196mph, and generate nearly 4g when cornering. The constructor was Dan Gurney's All American Racers.

What happened next

The DeltaWing's debut was at the 2012 Le Mans 24-hour race, and it was allowed to compete under experimental status ('Garage 56' category – anything goes, but for one year only). It retired after six hours on lap 75, after being struck by another car.

The next outing was the 1000-mile sports car race, the Petit Le Mans at Road Atlanta. During practice, it was again hit by another car. It came fifth in the race, having passed eight cars on the first lap. It completed 388 laps to the winner's 394. Ongoing development plans included a lighter, 2000cc, 345bhp engine, and a closed-top version for 2013.

Even conventional racing cars need constant fettling and finessing of cooling systems and spring rates, etc, and that such an unorthodox design came close to being right from day one is a remarkable achievement. Probably the only error of judgement was to succumb to the Batmobile comparison and paint it black, as early collisions were probably caused

by its near-stealth signature: to boldly go, indeed. All later version were in bright colours.

Manufacturers sponsor competition cars for the halo effect on their road cars, and after initial sponsorship and noteworthy press coverage, Nissan withdrew from the DeltaWing project.

But the story wasn't over

The DeltaWing camp's campaign continued, aimed at the American Le Mans Series style of races, using a Mazda-based 2000cc, 345bhp engine; its first race was at Austin.

A new, carbon-fibre tub was made, converting the design to a coupé, and the previously offset driving position to a central one. Apart from being a better driving position, the new superstructure protected the driver's head from flying crash debris, etc, and, if upside down at any stage, offered a more acceptable environment. For the 2014 season, weight had increased slightly to 9.65cwt (490kg).

Separately, Nissan continued its interest in Ben Bowlby's original motivation of fuel efficiency, creating with him the Nissan ZEOD RC (Zero Emissions on Demand Racing Car), a hybrid electric vehicle, to compete in the 2014 24-hour Le Mans. This coupé employed a new, 1500cc, three-cylinder, turbocharged engine, producing 400bhp, coupled with two 110kW electric motors, and employing regenerative braking. On electric cars or hybrids the electric motors driving the wheels can reverse to slow the car, and become generators that store battery power for later use.

The ZEOD RC achieved its goal of over 186mph on the Mulsanne Straight, and completed a lap on electric power alone. In the race, transmission failure forced its withdrawal.

THE DELTAWING CONCEPT WORKED WELL ENOUGH FOR DEVELOPMENT TO CONTINUE WITH A COUPÉ VERSION, AND A HYBRID ELECTRICAL VARIANT COMPETED IN THE 2014 LE MANS 24-HOUR RACE.

History will be the judge

It was suggested that the DeltaWing and ZEOD RC shared general visual characteristics. Both branches of this narrow-front-track tree aired proposals for road-going versions: one, a four-seater; one, a three-seater. Only time will tell whether this radical approach to a racing car layout will translate successfully to road use.

The entire concept may ultimately prove just an interesting experiment, but it immediately won an honorary place in the dare-to-be-different hall of fame.

Designer Ben Bowlby, when explaining the virtues of the super-lightweight DeltaWing, referred to its "mountain bike front springs."

Funny/shocking, practically a wrong-way-round-three-wheeler, even trumping the 1976 six-wheeler Tyrrell P34 in the initial 'You cannot be serious!' reaction stakes.

* * *

An endnote on motor racing from the only driver to win the 24 Hour Le Mans, Indianapolis 500, and Monaco Grand Prix – twice World Champion Graham Hill OBE: "It's like balancing an egg on a spoon while shooting the rapids."

Also from Graham Hull ...

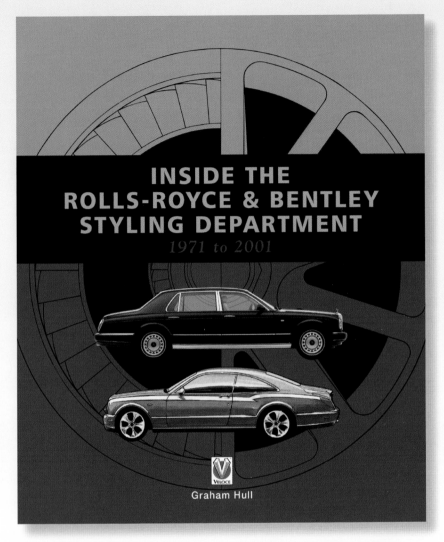

INSIDE THE
ROLLS-ROYCE & BENTLEY
STYLING DEPARTMENT
1971 to 2001

Graham Hull

A unique and personal account of a young designer's journey after joining
that most prestigious of marques, Rolls-Royce. Sometimes eccentric,
often humorous, the workings of this uniquely British institution during
a period of immense change are described in detail. Generously supported
by previously unseen illustrations, the author's story, from his position
as a designer and Chief Stylist, pulls back the curtain concealing an
idiosyncratic institution, motivated as much by pride as the bottom-line.

ISBN: 978-1-845846-01-5
Hardback • 25x20.7cm • £35* UK/$59.95* USA
• 176 pages • 100 colour and b&w pictures

For more info on Veloce titles, visit our website at www.veloce.co.uk
• email: info@veloce.co.uk • Tel: +44(0)1305 260068
* prices subject to change, p&p extra

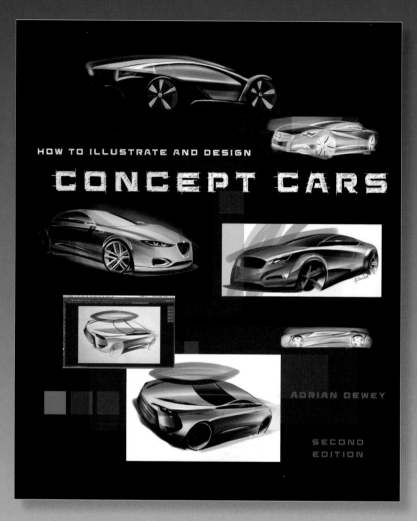

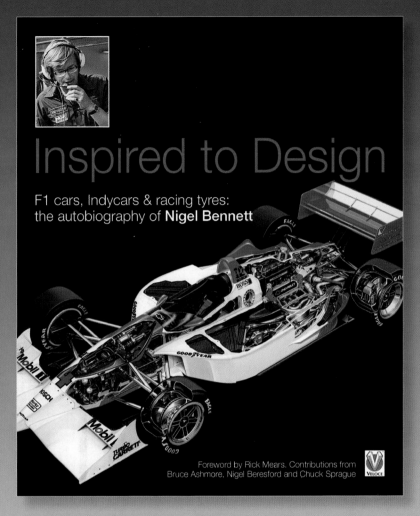

Inspired to Design

F1 cars, Indycars & racing tyres:
the autobiography of **Nigel Bennett**

Foreword by Rick Mears. Contributions from
Bruce Ashmore, Nigel Beresford and Chuck Sprague

Nigel Bennett's unique autobiography describes his life and career, from
growing-up influenced by car design, to his education and the building
of his 750 specials. He describes his work as Firestone Development
Manager, recounting many tales of the outstanding designers and drivers
of the period. Detailing his work in Formula 1, as a Team Lotus engineer,
and then as Team Ensign designer, he also covers his Indycar designs
at Theodore, Lola Cars and Penske Cars. Life after his retirement, his
involvement in boat design and with modern F1 teams, are also recounted.

ISBN: 978-1-845845-36-0
Hardback • 25x20.7cm • £35* UK/$54.95* USA
• 176 pages • 194 colour and b&w pictures

For more info on Veloce titles, visit our website at www.veloce.co.uk
• email: info@veloce.co.uk • Tel: +44(0)1305 260068
* prices subject to change, p&p extra

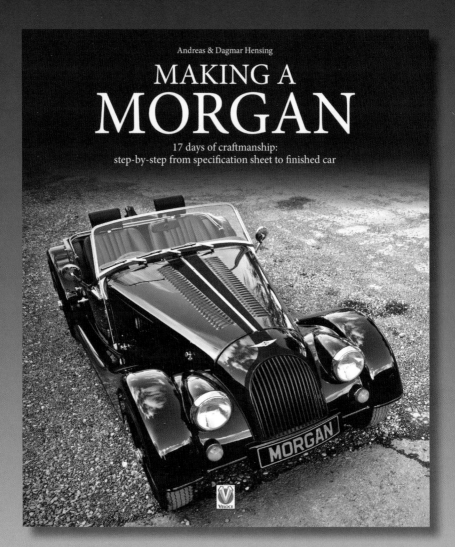

Index

Index